First World War
and Army of Occupation
War Diary
France, Belgium and Germany

34 DIVISION
102 Infantry Brigade
Northumberland Fusiliers
22nd Battalion (Tyneside Scottish)
10 January 1916 - 31 May 1918

WO95/2463/1

The Naval & Military Press Ltd
www.nmarchive.com
Published in association with The National Archives

Published by

The Naval & Military Press Ltd

Unit 10 Ridgewood Industrial Park,

Uckfield, East Sussex,

TN22 5QE England

Tel: +44 (0) 1825 749494

www.naval-military-press.com

www.nmarchive.com

This diary has been reprinted in facsimile from the original. Any imperfections are inevitably reproduced and the quality may fall short of modern type and cartographic standards.

© **Crown Copyright**
Images reproduced by permission of The National Archives, London, England, 2015.

Contents

Document type	Place/Title	Date From	Date To
Heading	WO95/2463 34 Division 102 Infantry Brigade Jan 1916-June 1918		
Heading	22nd Bn North'd Fus. Jan 1916-Jun 1918		
Heading	22nd Northumberland Fus. Vol I Jan 10th-30th		
War Diary	Warminster	10/01/1916	10/01/1916
War Diary	Havre	11/01/1916	12/01/1916
War Diary	Racquinghem	13/01/1916	23/01/1916
War Diary	Steenbecque	23/01/1916	01/02/1916
War Diary	Estaires	02/02/1916	02/02/1916
War Diary	Rouge De Bout	03/02/1916	07/02/1916
War Diary	Estaire	08/02/1916	08/02/1916
War Diary	Steenbecque	09/02/1916	13/02/1916
War Diary	Estaire	13/02/1916	16/02/1916
War Diary	Ref Map Sh 36. 64 Edition	17/02/1916	20/02/1916
War Diary	Rue Quesnoy	21/02/1916	25/02/1916
War Diary	Rue Dormoire	25/02/1916	29/02/1916
War Diary	Rue Dormoire Near Erquinghem	01/03/1916	08/03/1916
War Diary	Rue Marle Near Armentiere	08/03/1916	31/03/1916
War Diary	Map Ref. Sheet 36 Rue Marle Near Armentiere	01/04/1916	07/04/1916
War Diary	Rue Dormoire	07/04/1916	07/04/1916
War Diary	Vieux Berquin	08/04/1916	08/04/1916
War Diary	Morbecque	09/04/1916	09/04/1916
War Diary	Ref Map Sheet 36.a. Sheet 5.a. Hazebrouk Ebblinghem	10/04/1916	10/04/1916
War Diary	Ref Map Hazebrouk Sheet 5a	10/04/1916	10/04/1916
War Diary	Zudausques	11/04/1916	11/04/1916
War Diary	Nortleulinghem & Mentque	12/04/1916	06/05/1916
War Diary	Ref Amiens St Gratien	06/05/1916	10/05/1916
War Diary	Franvillers	10/05/1916	31/05/1916
War Diary	Franvillers	01/06/1916	01/06/1916
War Diary	Dernancourt	03/06/1916	03/06/1916
War Diary	Becourt Chateau	06/06/1916	06/06/1916
War Diary	Albert	15/06/1916	24/06/1916
War Diary	On Miguel	24/06/1916	25/06/1916
War Diary	Bresle	24/06/1916	30/06/1916
Operation(al) Order(s)	Operation Order No. 36 by Lt. Col. Elplinstone Commdg 3rd Tyneside Scottish	24/06/1916	24/06/1916
Heading	22nd Battalion Northumberland Fusiliers. (3rd Tyneside Scottish) July 1916		
War Diary	Assembly Trenches	01/07/1916	01/07/1916
War Diary	S. Of La Boiselle	01/07/1916	03/07/1916
War Diary	Usna-Tara Line	04/07/1916	04/07/1916
War Diary	Millencourt	05/07/1916	05/07/1916
War Diary	Pommier	06/07/1916	11/07/1916
War Diary	Warlincourt	11/07/1916	14/07/1916
War Diary	Lignereuil	15/07/1916	15/07/1916
War Diary	Bailleul-Aux-Cornailles	16/07/1916	16/07/1916
War Diary	Divion	16/07/1916	26/07/1916
War Diary	Maisnil Bouche	27/07/1916	27/07/1916
War Diary	Villers-Au-Bois	27/07/1916	31/07/1916
Heading	1/22nd Battalion Northumberland Fusiliers August 1916		

Type	Location/Description	Start	End
War Diary	Villiers-Au-Bois	01/08/1916	31/08/1916
War Diary	Bois Grenier Line	01/09/1916	30/11/1916
Heading	War Diary Dec 1916 22nd (s) Bn Northd Fus (3rd Tyneside Scottish) Vol 12		
War Diary	Bois Grenier Line	01/12/1916	12/01/1917
War Diary	Erquinghem	16/01/1917	16/01/1917
War Diary	Godewaersvelde	26/01/1917	31/01/1917
Heading	War Diary Of 22nd (S) Bn. Northd Fusiliers (3rd Tyneside Scottish) Month February 1917 Vol 14		
War Diary	Arras	02/03/1917	20/03/1917
War Diary	Roclincourt	23/03/1917	31/03/1917
Heading	War Diary April 1917. 22nd N.F. (3rd Tyneside Scottish) Northumberland Fus 102 Inf Bde Vol 16		
War Diary	'X' Huts Ecoivres Arras	01/04/1917	10/04/1917
War Diary	In the field Arras	10/04/1917	15/04/1917
War Diary	Moncht Breton	15/04/1917	23/04/1917
War Diary	Arras	23/04/1917	28/04/1917
War Diary	In the field Arras	28/04/1917	02/05/1917
War Diary	Hautville	03/05/1917	06/05/1917
War Diary	Sus St Leger	07/05/1917	07/05/1917
War Diary	Neuvilette	08/05/1917	08/05/1917
War Diary	Fienfillers	09/05/1917	30/05/1917
War Diary	Candas	30/05/1917	30/05/1917
War Diary	St Nicholas	30/05/1917	31/05/1917
War Diary	St Nicholas (Arras)	01/06/1917	04/06/1917
War Diary	Western Slope of Greenland Hill	05/06/1917	05/06/1917
War Diary	Greenland Hill	05/06/1917	07/06/1917
War Diary	St Nicholas	08/06/1917	11/06/1917
War Diary	Railway Cutting Point De Jour	11/06/1917	14/06/1917
War Diary	Greenland Hill	14/06/1917	17/06/1917
War Diary	Railway Cutting	17/06/1917	17/06/1917
War Diary	St Nicholas	20/06/1917	20/06/1917
War Diary	Arras	21/06/1917	21/06/1917
War Diary	Buneville	21/06/1917	04/07/1917
War Diary	Peronne	05/07/1917	05/07/1917
War Diary	Herville	05/07/1917	08/07/1917
War Diary	Villeret	09/07/1917	26/07/1917
War Diary	Bernes	26/07/1917	01/08/1917
War Diary	Vadencourt	02/08/1917	10/08/1917
War Diary	Barnes	11/08/1917	14/08/1917
War Diary	Villeret	15/08/1917	18/08/1917
War Diary	Hargicourt	19/08/1917	24/08/1917
War Diary	Hervilly	25/08/1917	25/08/1917
War Diary	Hargicourt	26/08/1917	31/08/1917
Miscellaneous	Patrol Scheme for the Night 3rd/4th August.	03/08/1917	03/08/1917
Miscellaneous	Patrol Scheme for the night 5th/6th August.		
Miscellaneous	Patrol Scheme for the night 6th/7th August.		
Miscellaneous	Patrol Scheme for the night 8th/9th August.		
Miscellaneous	Patrol Scheme for the night 9th/10th August.		
Miscellaneous	Patrol Scheme for the night 20th/21st August.	20/08/1917	20/08/1917
Miscellaneous	Patrol Scheme for the night 21st/22nd August.	21/08/1917	21/08/1917
Miscellaneous	Patrol Scheme for night 24th/25th August. by Major G Charlton Comdg. 22nd Bn Northumberland Fusiliers.	24/08/1917	24/08/1917
War Diary	Hargicourt	01/09/1917	02/09/1917
War Diary	Bernes	03/09/1917	07/09/1917
War Diary	Villaret	08/09/1917	12/09/1917

War Diary	Roisel	13/09/1917	17/09/1917
War Diary	Hargicourt	18/09/1917	25/09/1917
War Diary	Hancourt	26/09/1917	26/09/1917
War Diary	Doingt	27/09/1917	28/09/1917
War Diary	Bailleulval	29/09/1917	30/09/1917
Miscellaneous	Operation Orders No 141 by Major Gen Charlton Commdg. 22nd Bn Northld Fus		
War Diary	Bailleulval	01/10/1917	08/10/1917
War Diary	Poll Hill Camp	07/10/1917	12/10/1917
War Diary	Elverdinghe	13/10/1917	14/10/1917
War Diary	Langemarck	15/10/1917	16/10/1917
War Diary	Poelcappelle	17/10/1917	19/10/1917
War Diary	Langemarck	20/10/1917	24/10/1917
War Diary	Poll Hill Camp	25/10/1917	29/10/1917
War Diary	Northumberland Lines	30/10/1917	01/11/1917
War Diary	Guemappe York Lines M.2.2.b.9.3 (Ref Map Sheet 51b. S.W.)	05/11/1917	05/11/1917
War Diary	Battn. HQ Buck Reserve O.20.a.3.4	09/11/1917	09/11/1917
War Diary	Ref Map Sheet 51b S.W.	13/11/1916	13/11/1916
War Diary	Battn Hd Qrs O.20 A. 3.4 Buck Reserve	17/11/1916	30/11/1916
War Diary		01/12/1916	05/12/1916
War Diary	Btn H.Q. O20a 34	05/12/1916	09/12/1916
War Diary	York Lines (M22b 9.3)	10/12/1916	14/12/1916
War Diary	Henin Camp (N26 d40.20)	15/12/1916	31/12/1916
War Diary	Cuckoo Reserve O 25C.10.35.	01/01/1918	02/01/1918
War Diary	Shaft Avenue	03/01/1918	05/01/1918
War Diary	Cuckoo Reserve	06/01/1918	31/01/1918
War Diary	Northumberland Lines	01/02/1918	01/02/1918
War Diary	Mercatel	02/02/1918	08/02/1918
War Diary	Blairville	09/02/1918	09/02/1918
War Diary	Gouy en Artois	10/02/1918	10/02/1918
War Diary	Maizieres	11/02/1918	27/02/1918
War Diary	Berles Ervillers	28/02/1918	28/02/1918
Heading	22nd Battalion Northumberland Fusiliers March 1918		
War Diary	Belfast Camp	11/03/1918	21/03/1918
War Diary	U 25 B 55.25	21/03/1918	21/03/1918
War Diary	U 25a 6060	21/03/1918	22/03/1918
War Diary	Beaufort	25/03/1918	25/03/1918
War Diary	Villers L'Hopital	26/03/1918	27/03/1918
War Diary	Tannay	28/03/1918	28/03/1918
War Diary	Arrewage	28/03/1918	28/03/1918
War Diary	Estaires	30/03/1918	30/03/1918
War Diary	Erquinghem	31/03/1918	31/03/1918
Heading	22nd Battalion The Northumberland Fusiliers. April 1918		
War Diary	Erquingham	01/04/1918	05/04/1918
War Diary	Houplines	05/04/1918	11/04/1918
War Diary	Neippe	11/04/1918	11/04/1918
War Diary	Steenwerck	12/04/1918	13/04/1918
War Diary	Bailleul	14/04/1918	18/04/1918
War Diary	Mt Noir Nr Abeele	20/04/1918	20/04/1918
War Diary	St Jan Ker Biezen	22/04/1918	25/04/1918
War Diary	A.16.D	26/04/1918	30/04/1918
Heading	22nd Northumberland Fusiliers. May 1918		
War Diary	Brandhoek Line	01/05/1918	12/05/1918
War Diary	Zegers Cappel	12/05/1918	12/05/1918

War Diary	Lottinghem	13/05/1918	17/05/1918
War Diary	Becourt	18/05/1918	31/05/1918
Heading	22nd Northumberland Fusiliers. June 1918		
Miscellaneous	Cover for Documents. Nature of Enclosures. 102nd Bde Operation Orders TC		
Miscellaneous	34th Division Administrative Instructions No. 15		
Miscellaneous	Appendix "B" Programme For The Discharge Of Gas		
Miscellaneous	Appendix C		
Miscellaneous	Appendix C. Instruction For The Discharge Of Smoke.		

No. 95/2468

34 Division
102 Infantry Brigade.

Jan 1916 – June 1918

22 Battalion Northumberland Fusiliers

34TH DIVISION
102ND INFY BDE

22ND BN NORTH'D FUS.
JAN 1916 - FEB 1918.

To 16 DIV 48BDE

1a

22nd Northumb: Fus:
Vol: I
Jan 10th - 31st-

34th Div

Jan 16
Feb. 18

Army Form C. 2118.

WAR DIARY
or
INTELLIGENCE SUMMARY.
(Erase heading not required.)

22nd Northumberland Fusiliers

Instructions regarding War Diaries and Intelligence Summaries are contained in F. S. Regs., Part II. and the Staff Manual respectively. Title pages will be prepared in manuscript.

Place	Date	Hour	Summary of Events and Information	Remarks and references to Appendices
WARMINSTER	10.1.16	8.50AM	Bn. entrained in 3 trains at 2 hour intervals for SOUTHAMPTON	
HAVRE	11.1.16	7.AM	Bn. disembarked & marched to No.1 Base Camp. Distance about 4 miles	
"	12.1.16	12Noon	Bn. entrained in two trains.	
RACQUINGHEM	13.1.16		1st Train arrived BLENDECQUES 9.A.M. – Party marched off 11A.M. reached Billets at RACQUINGHEM at 1 P.M. Distance about 5 miles	
"	"		2nd " " WIZERNES at 2 P.M. – Party " 3 P.M. reached Billets at RACQUINGHEM at 6 P.M. Distance about 7 miles	
RACQUINGHEM	13.1.16 to 23.1.16		Bn. remained in same Billets.	
STEENBECQUE	23.1.16		Bn. marched off from RACQUINGHEM at 7.30AM and reached No 3 Camp STEENBECQUE at 11.45A.M. – Route BLARINGHEM – LES CISEAUX – STEENBECQUE – Distance about 8 miles.	
STEENBECQUE	23.1.16 to 31.1.16		Bn. remained in the same Camp.	

MWalkinton Lt. Col.
Comdg. 22nd Northn. Fus.

… Army Form C. 2118.

WAR DIARY or INTELLIGENCE SUMMARY.

(Erase heading not required.)

FEBRUARY.

Ref Map Sheet 36

Place	Date	Hour	Summary of Events and Information	Remarks and references to Appendices
STEEN-BECQUE	1.2.16		Bn. left Camp at STEENBECQUE & marched 16 Billets at ESTAIRES. Route — PONT LEVIS — LE PARC — LE PRÉ A VIN — CROSS ROADS K.15.C.4.2 — NEUF BERQUIN Hpt. Time 9 P.M. — 3.30 P.M. Distance about — 15 miles.	2/Lt Scott 16 NEUF BERQUIN Hpt. 1.2.16
ESTAIRES	2.2.16		Bn attacked for instruction 16 25th Bgd. Marched from ESTAIRE 3 P.M. reached billets around ROUGE DE BOUT in Bgd. Reserve area about 6 P.M. — Distance 6 miles. Route RUE DE LA LYS — Pt. DE LA JUSTICE — X roads G.35.a.8.8 — ROUGE DE BOUT. (Bgd. Front approx: N.8.B.O.0 16 N.4.C.95)	
ROUGE DES BOUT.	3.2.16		4 officers v N.C.O.'s A v B coys in trenches with right Bn. 2/Rifle Bgd. Morning 16 evening	
			" " " C v D " " " " 2/Lincolns " "	
			" " " A v B " " " " 1/R Irish Rifles Evening " Afternoon 4.2.16
			" " " C v D " " left " 2/Rifle Bgd. " " 4.2.16
			" " " " " " " 2/R. Berks. R. " " 4.2.16
	4.2.16		2 Platoons A v B " " right " 1/R Irish Rifles " 4th " Evening 5.2.16
			" " C v D " " left " 2/R Berks. R " 4.2.16 " 5.2.16
	5.2.16		" " A v B " " right " 1/Irish Rifles " 5.2.16 "
			" " C v D " " left " 2/R. Berks " 5.2.16 "
	6.2.16		A Coy " " Right " 1/Irish Rifles " 6.2.16 " Evening 7.2.16
			C Coy " " Left " 2/R. Berks " 6.2.16 " 7.2.16
	7.2.16		B Coy " " Right " 2/Rifle Bgd. " 7.2.16 " Evening 8.2.16
			D Coy " " Left " 2/Lincolns " 7.2.16 " 8.2.16

Casualties 1/2/16 — 8/2/16 Feb

1 Pte A Coy slightly wounded at duty.
Capt: S.J.S. Bolt slightly wounded returned 16 duty 10.2.16
Capt: J. Mann to coy Alexandra Hotel Oliedin Hosp 8.2.16
Capt: R Clay Concussion from shell burst — Returned 11.2.16

WAR DIARY
or
INTELLIGENCE SUMMARY.
(Erase heading not required.)

Army Form C. 2118.

Instructions regarding War Diaries and Intelligence Summaries are contained in F.S. Regs., Part II. and the Staff Manual respectively. Title pages will be prepared in manuscript.

Place	Date	Hour	Summary of Events and Information	Remarks and references to Appendices
ESTAIRE	8.2.16		Bn marched back to billets in ESTAIRE by Coys. Last Coy in billets by 6.45 P.M.	
STEENBECQUE	9.2.16	9.30 P.M	Bn. marched off at 9.30 P.M. reached camp in STEENBECQUE about 4 P.M.	Capt. Mc.CLAY readmitted to Hosp. 12-2-16
STEENBECQUE	9.2.16 to 13.2.16		Bn in camp at STEENBECQUE.	2/Lt. SCOTT rejoined from Hosp. 12-2-16
ESTAIRE	13.2.16		The Bn marched with 102nd Bgd to ESTAIRE - Route as on 1.2.16 marched off 9.15 A.M. Arrived 3.30 P.M.	2/Lt. BOSGROVE to Bgd TRENCH MORTAR BATTERY
	14.2.16		102nd Bgd took over trenches from 25th and were attached to 8th Div. Bgd Front - N.8.3 to N.10.5 (Ref. French Maps) - N.2.9.0 16 and N.d.8.0 (Ref Map 36. 6th Position) Bn took over [from] centre section N.10.1 to N.10.6 (" ") - N.10.C.0.6 15 N.10.d.8.0 (" " " ") holding B. Sadline from to 2 BERKSHIRE RGT	
			The 21st Manch Fus holding right section was on right flank. The 2nd Bn Yorks and Lancs " " " Left " Bn. Head Quarters at Point N.8. B. 2. 3. Bn. march from ESTAIRE via BAILLEY - ROUGE ROUT - LA CROIX LE SCOMMES at 3.15 P.M. Relief completed at 8.25 P.M.	
	15.2.16 16.2.16		Bn held trenches as above. Both days very quiet; on night of 15th our artillery bombarded enemy lines from 9 P.M. to 9.30 P.M. - On night of 16th 11.10 P.M. to 11.30 P.M. On both occasions enemy retaliated with its artillery & trench mortar fire. No Casualties.	

WAR DIARY
or
INTELLIGENCE SUMMARY.
(Erase heading not required.)

Army Form C. 2118.

(4)

Place	Date	Hour	Summary of Events and Information	Remarks and references to Appendices
Ref. Map Sh. 36. 614. Pelette	17.2.16		Bn relieved by 23rd North Fus. and occupied their billets in Bgd. Reserve area. 1 Coy (D) in Close support to front line at CROIX BLANCHE. Head Quarters JERRY VILLA M.26.d.4-7. Our guides met Platoons of 23rd at 6 P.M. at CROIX BLANCHE. Relief completed at 9.55 P.M.	Casualties 17.2.16 Killed 7789 C. Delaney Pte. (accidentally) wounded 2/9. Anderson Pte. (accidentally) 1500 B. Hardy " (shell same class) 1308 P.Martin " 612 J. Fox (shell 19.2.16)
	18.2.16 to 20.2.16		2nd North. Fus. in Bgd. Reserve on our right. H.Q. ROUGE DE BOUT (9.36.c.8.7) Bn remained in Bgd. Reserve in same billets.	2Lt. Stott 10 HpLt 19.2.16
RUE QUESNOY	21.2.16		Bn relieved by 2/Bgd Bombs and went each to Div. Reserve. Bn less D Coy. marched off at 5.40 P.M. Route – M.26.d.11 – M.26.a.11 – H.19.b.4.o. to Billets on RUE QUESNOY. Bn. H.Q. H.19.c.o.8.	24.2.16 Killed Pte Cole.
	21.2.16 to 25.2.16		Relief of D Coy completed 6.55 P.M. Bn in same billets.	
	25.2.16		102nd Bgd relieved 68th Inf Bgd in 34th Div. area. & rejoined to 34th Div. Bn marched at 2 P.M. & took over billets from 11th North. Fus handing over to 13th D.L.I.	
RUE DORMOIRE	25.2.16 to 29.2.16		ROUTE # 13.c.69 – FORT ROMPU – RUE DORMOIRE (Brulé) Bn in Divisional Reserve in same Billets.	

W Welchman Lt Col., Comdg.
22nd North. Fus.

REF.MAP.SHEET - 36 c Edition.6.

Army Form C. 2118.

WAR DIARY
or
INTELLIGENCE SUMMARY.
(Erase heading not required.) 22nd NORTHD FUS: 3rd T.S

Place	Date	Hour	Summary of Events and Information	Remarks and references to Appendices
RUE. DORMOIRE  ERQUINGHEM	1.3.16		Bn in Billets in Divisional Reserve, Hd.Qrs. M.8.b.9.3	1.3.16 Capt. WILLIAMS Bombing is Hospital
"	1.3.16 to 4.3.16		Bn. in Same Billets	
"	4.3.16		Tr 102nd Bgd relieved the 103rd Bgd. the 22nd N.F. taking over Fond line trench from I.24.d. Northd. Fus (Trenches. Trench Ref. I.25.5./5. I.21.2 exclusive) Bn. H.Q.s. I.21.a.b.4.0	4.3.16 4 to 2/Lt Harden killed Pte Rolf wounded
"	4.3.16 to 8.3.16		Two Coys held the front line. A.B.C from the right. D coy in support in Bois GRENIER LINE. A marked patient in left sector of front trench, at points only 50 to 60 yds from the enemy parapet. The 23rd North. Fus held line on our left. 16th Royal Scots " " " right.	1 Cpl. 2 2/Cpls 7 Privates (3 of above W-Daily)
"	8.3.16		On the 5th 6th the enemy artillery was fairly active, but with snowy weather on the 7th 8th practically stopped all activity. Owing to bad weather the trenches were in a few condition much work in strengthening & restabilising parapet was carried out. 15000 Sand bags were used. At night the 8th our men were wounded whilst patrolling in front of the Parapet.	5.3.16. Draft of 20 O.R joined 8.3.16 CAPTAIN WILLIAMS Returned to Bn duty.

Army Form C. 2118.

WAR DIARY
or
INTELLIGENCE SUMMARY.
(Erase heading not required.)

(6)

Place	Date	Hour	Summary of Events and Information	Remarks and references to Appendices
RUE MARLE near ARMENTIERE	8.3.16		Bn relieved by the 21st North. Fus and marched back to their billets in Bgd Reserve. Relief was completed at 9.35 A.M. Distribution of Coy's & H.Q. H.Q. — RUE MARLE H.6.a.8.8. C. Coy — B Coy — L'ARMEE A. Coy — CHAPELLE ARMENTIERE D. Coy — Trenches in BOIS GRENIER LINE (I.15.b.3.3)	Casualties 9.3.16 wounded 1 Cpl (Sinclair) & 3 Privates.
			Scheme in case of attack. Bn to occupy BOIS GRENIER LINE From Right of Bgd area to LILLE ROAD	11.3.16 H. ATKINSON proceeded to WISCHES for M.G. Course 13.3.16
	9.3.16.		A Coys billets shelled in afternoon 1 Cpl & 3 men wounded	
	10.3.16.		On account of Shelling of their billets, A Coy was moved up to the BOIS GRENIER LINE & accommodated in trenches in rear of D (I.19.c)	
	11.3.16		Wintry type of weather changed and became much more favourable for operations.	CAPTAIN AMOS 2/M. SMITH Joined the Bn for duty
	14.3.16.		Bn took over same line of trenches from the 21st N.F. Coys in same positions as before. Relief commenced 11. P.M. Completed at 1 AM.	Casualties 15th Worth. Fus. Left Flank — 23rd North Fus. 15th 1.O.R wounded Right Flank — 27th 16th 1.O.R. " by STOKES 17th " guns 1. L.Cpl Killed 2. O.R Wounded
	16.3.16		A Bombardment of enemy Salient was carried out in afternoon	

WAR DIARY or INTELLIGENCE SUMMARY

Army Form C. 2118.

Place	Date	Hour	Summary of Events and Information	Remarks and references to Appendices
	17.3.16		and artillery. Our Scout Corporal & another unoccupied ws found to have been shelled.	18.3.16 1. O.R. wounded
	18.3.16		Heavy rifle and M.G. fire during night. 3 casualties.	18.3.16 Lieut. ATKINSON v Capt. McCLAY Rejoined
	19.3.16		2nd Draft of 20 Rein Personnel joined. Enemy Artillery fairly Active.	
	20.3.16		" " " Again Active. In the Salient the road Coy had been Rrd. line parapets shelled by 21st Nott. Fus. and marched back to ESTAMINET. and the Centre evening in the H.Q. RUE MAPLE. H.6.d.8.8. Relieved 2 Coys WEST of RUE MAPLE. in 2 " H.5. & 9.7. Billets. Relief commenced at 7.30 P.M and was completed 10.20 P.M.	Casualties 20.3.16 5. O.R. wounded of which one 2nd Lieut M.Donaldson are remained at duty
	20.3.16 25.9.16		The Bn remained in Bgd. Reserve in above Billets.	2nd Draft of 20 m on reported for duty. (19.3.16)

WAR DIARY
INTELLIGENCE SUMMARY.
(Erase heading not required.)

Army Form C. 2118.

Place	Date	Hour	Summary of Events and Information	Remarks and references to Appendices
	25.3.16.		Bn again went forward to the 1st Line and 166th over Para Lines of trenches from to 21st North Fire. Distribution of Coys. A. Right. B. Centre & C. Support. D. Left.	Casualties 25-30. Killed. 1 Lcpl. 3 Privates. Wounded C.S.M. Falkener 1 Cpl. 11 Privates.
	28.3.16		Artillery and trench Mortar scheme Carried out against German parapet - parapets opposite paticed (t.s/s).	2nd Lt. E. ASHLEY joined on 28th T.
	29.3.16		Weather favourable for observation and artillery fairly active - a considerable number of Prisoners - in right Coy.	
	30.3.16		Again relieved by 21st North Fus. and took over billets & Posts in Bgd Reserve as under. H.Q. & A Coy RUE MAPLE. D Coy L'ARMEÉ. B Coy less 1½ Platoons about H.12.6.4.7. x 1 Platoon at FME au BIEZ x 1 " " PARADISE ALLEY x C Coy in Bois GRENIER LINE from HAYSTACH AV. to LILLE ROAD. x All under trench conditions.	2/Lt W.D CLAYTON joined 1½ bn on the 31st.
	31.3.16		In Billets.	

W Tulin Cpt.
p.Col.
22nd N.F.

22 Nov Feb 4a
Vol 4

Army Form C. 2118.

SHEET -9-

XXXIV

WAR DIARY
or
INTELLIGENCE SUMMARY.
(Erase heading not required.)

Instructions regarding War Diaries and Intelligence Summaries are contained in F. S. Regs., Part II. and the Staff Manual respectively. Title pages will be prepared in manuscript.

Place	Date	Hour	Summary of Events and Information	Remarks and references to Appendices
MAP Ref. Sheet 36				
RUE MARLE near ARMENTIERE	1.4.16		Bn. in Bgd. Reserve. Distribution.	
			Bn. HQ - A. Coy at RUE MARLE.	
			D " " L'ARMEE	
			C " " BOIS GRENIER LINE (Trenches).	
			2 Platoon B " H. 12.6 - 4.7 (Billets.)	
			" " " FME DU BIEZ (I.15.b.3.5.) & PARADISE ALLEY (Trenches).	
	1.4.16 to 7.4.16		Bn. in same area.	
RUE DORMOIRE			On the night 7/8 April Bn. was relieved by the 25th Australian Infantry Bn, and 16th over Rivers from the 27th Australian Infantry Bn.	
			Bn. H.Q. RUE DORMOIRE H.9.6.5.9	
VIEUX BERQ. -VIN	8.4.16		Bn marched off at 8.30 AM & went into new billets - on either sides of Road 5 of VIEUX BERQUIN at 1 P.M.	
			ROUTE - BHP ST MAUR -	
			CROIX DU BAC	Rep. Maps.
			LE CRUSABEAU	Sheets 36 & 36a 1/40000
			DOULIEU	Distances about 12 miles.
			L.3.C.6.5	
			F.19.6.6.2	
			Bn. H.Q. - 1K.30.a.9.0.	

Army Form C. 2118.

WAR DIARY
or
INTELLIGENCE SUMMARY.   SHEET. 10.
(Erase heading not required.)

Instructions regarding War Diaries and Intelligence Summaries are contained in F.S. Regs., Part II. and the Staff Manual respectively. Title pages will be prepared in manuscript.

Place	Date	Hour	Summary of Events and Information	Remarks and references to Appendices
MAP Ref. Sheet. 36.a 1/40.000.				
MORBECQUE	9.4.16		Bn marched off 8.30 A.M. reached Billets near MORBECQUE at 12 NOON. ROUTE. LA MOTTE X roads X Roads D.24.a.10 PAPOTTE Rd Junction D.21.d.6.8. Bn. H.Q. D.13.a.8.1	Distance about 8 miles.
Ref. Map. Sheet. 36.a. Sheet. 5.a. Hazebrouck EBBLINGHEM	10.4.16		Marched off 8.30 reached billets in EBBLINGHEM at 1 P.M. ROUTE { C.28.c.6.4.9 B.12. C.6.3 } Sheet 36.a B.2. 8.36 RENESCURE } Sheet 5.A. EBBLINGHEM Bn. H.Q. at Ho HAMLE - EBBLINGHEM.	Distance about 10 miles.
Ref. Map. HAZEBROUK Sheet. 6.A. ZUDAUSQUES	11.4.16		Marched off 8. AM reached billets in ZUDAUSQUES 1 PM ROUTE ARQUES TATINGHEM ZUDAUSQUES Bn. H.Q. Ho HAMLE ZUDAUSQUES	Distance about 12 miles.

WAR DIARY
or
INTELLIGENCE SUMMARY.
(Erase heading not required.)

Army Form C. 2118.

SHEET 11

Instructions regarding War Diaries and Intelligence Summaries are contained in F. S. Regs., Part II. and the Staff Manual respectively. Title pages will be prepared in manuscript.

Place	Date	Hour	Summary of Events and Information	Remarks and references to Appendices
Ref. Maps B Series Sheets 27.A.1/20.000		N.E S.E.		
NORTLEULINGHEM & MENTQUE	12.4.16		Bn marched off 10. PM reached new Billets a/-12.30 P.M. ROUTE. W.1.B. 8.1 Distance about 5 miles Q.25.c. 8.6 Road very hilly. P.18.a. 9.6 MENTQUE Head Qrs - FARM R.5.a.1.3. A.B.&C. Coys NORTLEULINGHEM D Coy MENTQUE	26-4-16 2/Lt MASON loaned for duty
	13.4.16		Rest.	
	14.4-16 to 30.4-16		Platoon Training - Coy Training - Bn... Bayonet & Divisional Training Bn remained in same Billets".	

W.W.Wilkinson
Crg. 2ⁿᵈ Ironside Leather
22ⁿᵈ Inn?? Inv.

Lieut-Coll Acting
22ⁿᵈ ?? N.F.

Army Form C. 2118.

WAR DIARY
of
INTELLIGENCE SUMMARY.
(Erase heading not required.)

Sheet 12

Instructions regarding War Diaries and Intelligence Summaries are contained in F. S. Regs., Part II. and the Staff Manual respectively. Title pages will be prepared in manuscript.

Place	Date	Hour	Summary of Events and Information	Remarks and references to Appendices
Ref. Maps. B.Sario Sub 27 A. 1/40,000 NE " " S.E				
NORTHEUVLINGHEM & MENTQUE	1·5·16		Platoon training. Company training. Batt. Brigade & Divisional training	
	6·5·16		Battalion remained in same billets.	
Ref. AMIENS – 17 ST GRATIEN			At 2·43 am on the 6th Battalion entrained at St OMER for LONGEAU arriving at latter place 11·45am: Marched to St GRATIEN via AMIENS 9. reached billets at 6·0 pm, 6th. Route via AMIENS & ALLONVILLE – distance, 11 miles	10·5·16 Maj. AIRLOM joined the Bn
	6·5·16 to 10·5·16		Battalion remained in same billets.	
FRANVILLERS	10·5·16		Bn marched at 6.30 P.M and went mile new billets at FRANVILLERS. Route FRECHENCOURT – BEHENCOURT. Distance about 5. MILES.	
	11·5·16		Bn remained in same billets. Bess A. Coy moved to ALBERT.	

22 Middx Regt

WAR DIARY or INTELLIGENCE SUMMARY

Army Form C. 2118.

XXXIV SHEET 13 VOL 5

Place	Date	Hour	Summary of Events and Information	Remarks and references to Appendices
FRANVILLERS	14.5.16		D Coy relieved A Coy in ALBERT.	17.5.16 2/Lt A.D.GIBSON " N. PETERS " C. PIEGROME " H.W. MOLE Joined the Bn
	15.5.16		B " proceeded to ALBERT.	
	19.5.16		A & C Coys relieved D & B Coys at ALBERT.	Casualties
	23.5.16		D & B " A & C " "	21.5.16 1Pte wounded. 23.5.16 1" killed (self inflicted) 26.5.16 1" wounded 28.5.16 1" killed 30.5.16 # Cosgrove killed accidentally 31.5.16 Pte Davis wounded 1Pte wounded
	27.5.16 to 31.5.16		A & C " D & B " " Bn. H.Q. still at FRANVILLERS and the dispositions of the Battalion unchanged.	10.5.16 Maj. ACKLOM joined the Bn

W Wills Capt. Actg.
22nd North'n R.

A.K.Alphonse Lt Col.
Comdg. 22nd North'n Reg

WAR DIARY
or
INTELLIGENCE SUMMARY.
(Erase heading not required.)

Army Form C. 2118.

SHEET (14) 22nd Northumberland

Place	Date	Hour	Summary of Events and Information	Remarks and references to Appendices
FRANVILLERS	1.6.16		H.Q. B & D Coy's in FRANVILLERS. C & A Coy's in ALBERT	Casualties Wounded

DERNANCOURT	3.6.16		On night of 3/4 June Bn. moved into forward area and June 2nd — 1 O.R
			relieved the 11th SUFFOLKS as under. 4th — 1 "
			H.Q. B & D Coys to DERNANCOURT 5th — 1 "
			A & C Coys to BECOURT (CHATEAU. (3 at duty) 2. O.R
			On night of 3/4th a hostile raid was attempted 6th Killed
			its right Sector held by 21st N.F. against 10th — 12 Wounded
			  (1 at duty)
			  (1 duty in Hosp)
			On night of 5/6th June 2 Bn. from DERNANCOURT was moved up. 11th — 2. O.R. wounded
			H.Q. & D Coy to CHATEAU & came under 14th — 1 "
			B Coy right forward section & orders of O.C. 21st N.F. (at duty)

BECOURT CHATEAU	6.6.16		On night of 6/7th June the Bn. relieved the 21st N.F. and 10th on night. trenches from X.20.6 on left to ABERDEEN AV. X.20.1 on right. (Trench map. Ref.) body marched about - Don Right. Trenches especially on right V central C. Centre. a lot of work day on left & on rep/air on B. Left. subsided. 23rd N.F on our left & on Right A KOYLI

WAR DIARY
or
INTELLIGENCE SUMMARY.
(Erase heading not required.)

Sheet (13)

Army Form C. 2118.

Place	Date	Hour	Summary of Events and Information	Remarks and references to Appendices
ALBERT	15th June		On 10th June (afternoon) Bn was relieved by 21st N.F. and took over the Defences of BECOURT WOOD. H.Q. at BECOURT CHATEAU. On night of 14/15th June Bn was relieved by 15th Royal Scots. Club. 16.21st N.F. & proceeded to Billets as under. H.Q. B. Coy D. Coy } ALBERT A. Coy C. Coy } Camp E.6.6.6.1 (Ref. Map. ALBERT, Combined Sheet.)	14.6.16. Lt. BIRBY on MEGPHONE attached to N.F. MAJOR APPLON for Special Duty to 102nd Bdes.
	16th June		On night of 16/17th June Bn relieved the 20th N.F. in the Left Section & took over trenches from X.13.6 16 x 20.6 (Trench Ref.) A. Right. { 15th Royal Scots on Right. B. Left. { 2nd Devons on Left. C. Support. D. 2 Platoon with A. 2 Platoon at USNA REDOUBT.	

WAR DIARY
or
INTELLIGENCE SUMMARY.
(Erase heading not required.)

Army Form C. 2118.

Sheet 16

Place	Date	Hour	Summary of Events and Information	Remarks and references to Appendices
16ᵃ	16 24ᵗʰ June.		The Bn. held the trenches as shown on P.H.17 (15) Trenches very much crowded with carrying parties lined up loin for future movement. On night of 22/23 25 men were gased while on on gas cylinders were being placed in front and line	2ⁿᵈ A.D.G.P.O. Belmullies 16 HPU on 19ᵗʰ
on Night 24/25 June.			Bn. was relieved by 1 Coy 18ᵗʰ Pioneers 8 Platoon 20ᵗʰ M.F. & 5 Platoon ＶＨＱ of 23ʳᵈ M.F. After Bn. marched back to R. billets in BAIZIEUX Casualties.	CAPTAIN AMOS admitted to HPU on 22ⁿᵈ
			18.6.16. — 10 O.R. wounded. 19.6.16 — 6 O.R. " 21.6.16 — 1 O.R. killed 4 O.R. wounded. 22.6.16 — 17 O.R. killed 21 O.R. wounded.	

Army Form C. 2118.

SHEET 17

WAR DIARY
or
INTELLIGENCE SUMMARY.
(Erase heading not required.)

Place	Date	Hour	Summary of Events and Information	Remarks and references to Appendices
BRESLE	24–26th		The Battalion remained in trenches at BRESLE	
	25/26th		2 Platoons proceeded to USNA-TARA line	
	26/27th		6 Platoons proceeded to SUNKEN GARDEN ALBERT	
	27/28th		6 Platoons proceeded to USNA-TARA line from SUNKEN GARDEN.	
	28/29th		2 Companies proceeded to FORWARD TRENCHES from USNA TARA LINE	
	29/30th		2 Companies proceeded to USNA-TARA line from BRESLE. A bombing party consisting of 2 officers and 20 men proceeded towards the enemy lines with a view to raiding them. The party were unable to reach the enemy trenches owing to heavy fire but all returned safely to our lines.	Casualties 2nd Lt McDonald wounded. Killed. 4. Wounded. 12. Missing 3
	30th		The Battalion remained in position in the line, in support to the 21st N.F. The 20th N.F and 23rd N.F were in position on the LEFT, the 101st BDE. were in position on the RIGHT. – By 10.30 p.m. all companies of the Battn were distributed in their assembly trenches for the attack tomorrow morning at 7.60 a.m.	

commdg:- Benen Allison Major

3rd BATTALION TYNESIDE SCOTTISH,
(22nd (S) Bn. NORTHD. FUS:)

REF: Map LA BOISSELLE
1:5000.

24.6.16

Operation Order No 36
by Lt. Col. Elphinstone
Commdg. 3rd Tyneside Scottish.

1. **Intention** In conjunction with remainder of
III Corps the 34th Division is to make
an attack on the German position.
Operations will extend over 6 days,
which will be known as U V W X Y Z.
The preliminary bombardment, including
smoke & gas, will extend over the
first 5 days.
The infantry assault will take
place on Z day.

2. **Troops** The 34th Div. will be on the RIGHT.
" 8th " " " " " LEFT
" 19th " " " " in RESERVE

The 34th Div. is being disposed for
the attack as under:—
    102nd Bgde on LEFT
    101st " " RIGHT
    103rd " in RESERVE

The 102nd Bgde. will advance in
two columns:—
    RIGHT COLUMN: 2nd T.S. supported by 3rd T.S.
    LEFT " : 1st T.S. " " 4th T.S.

O.O.36 — 2

3. Objective of 102nd Bgde

1st OBJECTIVE — German trenches up to and including line from
X.9.c.6.3 to X.15.b.4.2

2nd OBJECTIVE — Line from
X.10.a.6.5 to X.16.b.1.6

1st & 2nd T.S. will capture & consolidate 1st Objective

3rd & 4th T.S. will capture & consolidate 2nd Objective.

The particular front to be captured and consolidated by the 22nd N.F. is from X.10.c.5.3 to X.16.b.1.5 taking in the whole of CONTALMAISON WOOD.

4. Position of Assembly

The Bn. will assemble on Y/Z night into assembly trenches previously prepared as under:—

1st Line: Along DUNDEE AVENUE — left resting on point where MERCIER ST. joins

2nd Line: ALNWICK STREET

3rd Line: Along DUNDEE AVENUE with right resting on point where MERCIER ST. joins

4th Line: New trench dug from junction of BUDDON ST. and DUNDEE AVE.

Order from right to left
A
B
C
D

Each line will consist of one platoon of each Coy. drawn up from right to left in order as per margin

O. O. 36 – 3

5. LA BOISSELLE. Prior to the assault 2 platoons of D. Coy. and 1 Lewis Gun under 2/Lt W.H.Robson will come under orders of O.C. Bgde. Bombing Coy. to assist in clearing LA BOISELLE. After this has been accomplished, they will, together with half the Bombing Coy., re-join the Bn. at the 2nd Objective.

6. Advance. The Bn., less 2 platoons of D. Coy., and 1 Lewis Gun, will advance on a front and depth of four platoons at 2 paces interval and 150 yds. distance; Coys. being distributed from right to left as under —

    RIGHT :   A
    RIGHT CENTRE : B
    LEFT CENTRE :   C
    LEFT :   D

1st Line:
1 platoon each Coy.

2nd Line:
1 platoon A, B, & C. Coys.

3rd Line:
1 platoon A, B, & C. Coys.

4th Line:
1 platoon each Coy.

They will then form four lines as per margin.

The remaining 7 Lewis Guns will advance intermingled with the rear platoons of their respective Coys.

Half bombers A & B. Coys. will march on right flank of Bn., & half bombers C. & D on left flank of Bn., remaining bombers with platoons.

The leading line will follow the 2nd T.S. at an interval of 150 yds.

O.O. 36 - 4.

7. Line of Advance. The right of the Bn. will cross over our first line trench at point X.20.a.5.1, and march on south corner of CONTALMAISON WOOD. True compass bearing 60°. A. Coy. will direct.

A slight detour must be made so as to leave German trench from point 83 to point 05 on our right.

8. Consolidation. On arrival at final objective the position will be consolidated as follows:-

A. Coy. (less 1 platoon) will consolidate and hold German trench from road just W. of point 18 (inclusive) to point 27, forming a strong point for 2 platoons at the latter point.

B. Coy. (less 1 platoon) will consolidate and hold German trench from left of A to a point in rear of centre of CONTALMAISON WOOD, forming a strong point at 99.

C. Coy. (less 1 platoon) will consolidate and hold the N.E. edge of CONTALMAISON WOOD.

1 Platoon D. Coy.
Will reverse and hold German trench from point 63 towards B. Coy.

The remaining platoons comprising

O.O. 36 – 5

4th Line will be disposed by order of the C.O. as the situation may demand.

9. <u>Connection</u>. On reaching the Objective, A. Coy. will be responsible for at once getting into touch with the 101st Bgde. at points X.16.b.2.4 and X.16.b.2.3. D. Coy. for getting into touch with H4th T.S.

10. <u>Zero Hour</u>. The hour of ZERO will be notified later.
At 8 minutes before ZERO hurricane bombardment will be opened.
At 2 minutes before ZERO, 2 lines of the 2nd T.S. will advance over the parapet, and 3rd T.S. will follow, occupying the trenches vacated by them.

11. <u>Instructions</u>. Matters of dress, equipment, and other details, are dealt with in instructions issued in conjunction with these orders.

O.O. 36 - 6

12. Evacuation of Wounded — Reg¹ Aid Post will be established at junction of GOWRIE STREET and METHUEN STREET.
Wounded will be evacuated by GOWRIE STREET and PERTH AVE. to A.D.S. of KINFAUNS ST — PERTH AVE.

13. Reports

Bgde. H.Q. are at W.24.b.5.1 and after advance will move to X.14.d.1.9 in LA BOISSELLE
Bn. H.Q. will be in rear of the centre of the 4ᵗʰ wave during the advance, and on reaching the final objective in the vicinity of road junction X.16.a.2.8

14. Papers etc.

With the exception of French Map 1/5000 and map sheet 57ᴰ S.E. 1/20.000 no orders or papers will be taken into action.

W Tubb Capt
Adjt
22ⁿᵈ North Fus

102nd Bde.
34th Div.

****
Brigade temporarily transferred
to 37th Division 6th July –
Rejoined 34th Division 22nd August.
****

22ⁿᵈ BATTALION

NORTHUMBERLAND FUSILIERS.

(3ᴰ Tyneside Scottish)

JULY 1916.

WAR DIARY
or
INTELLIGENCE SUMMARY.

3rd BATTALION TYNESIDE SCOTTISH
(22nd (S) Bn. NORTHD. FUS:)

Army Form C. 2118.

SHEET 18 — Vol 7

(Erase heading not required.)

Place	Date	Hour	Summary of Events and Information	Remarks and references to Appendices
ASSEMBLY TRENCHES	1/7/1916	7:30 AM	The Battalion together with the 21ST NORTHD FUS; forming the Right assaulting column moved forward to the attack on the enemy trenches S. of LA BOISELLE. Heavy enemy fire was experienced but the Bn less heavy casualties suffered reached ENEMY 2ND LINE	Appendium also attached.
		8.0 AM	A small party proceeded towards the ENEMY 3RD LINE but had to return owing to heavy enemy fire, several casualties were suffered. MAJOR ACKLOM R.A. by this time taken command owing to LT. COL. ELPHINSTONE having become a casualty. RIGHT FLANK of position held in ENEMY 2ND LINE extended to small party of LINCOLNS trenches strengthened. Six separate attempts to rush our flanks were made by the enemy without avail	
		12.45 pm	Shrapnel 7 OFFICERS and 200 other ranks, a mixture of remnants of 22nd and 21st NF of which MAJOR ACKLOM R.A. taken command of the battalion in the Brigade	
		10.15 pm	At dusk got in touch with other troops in the NEW CRATER, caused by our mine, 100 yds beyond our right flank	
S. of LA BOISELLE	2/7/1916	—	ALL RANKS greatly in need of water and very much fatigued. CONSOLIDATION of position continued slowly.	
		3.30 am	CHESHIRES arrived in our lines preparing for further advance.	
		4.25 am	Enemy bombarded position with 5.9's	
		10.5 am	Enemy shelling slightly moderated	
		2.40 pm	ordered to hold position at ALL COSTS. LINCOLNS and R. WELSH FUS arrived in our lines	
		5.10 pm	Two LEWIS guns returned and placed in position	
		7.0 pm	THREE VICKERS guns returned — placed in position	
		11.55 pm	Two stokes guns received + placed in position. Plentiful supply of water + rations received. Men in good spirits. POSITION SECURE	

WAR DIARY or INTELLIGENCE SUMMARY

3rd BATTALION TYNESIDE SCOTTISH
(22nd (S) Bn. NORTHD. FUS.)

SHEET. 19.

Army Form C. 2118.

Place	Date	Hour	Summary of Events and Information	Remarks and references to Appendices
H.Q. LA BOISELLE	July 2/3rd mid-night		STRENGTH - 5 OFFICERS and 155 NCO's and men.	Casualties from 1st – 3rd July
	July 3.	12 NOON.	2 more OFFICERS joined the Casualties reported for duty.	OFFICERS KILLED 7
			LIEUT ROTHERFORD and CPL. BURNS carried out a careful reconnaissance of the ground beyond our RIGHT FLANK under heavy machine gun fire. This was to select a route for a party to connect up with the troops on our RIGHT.	Lt. W. Elphinstone. Major Sillwill. Capt. Tulli. Capt. Laing. Capt. Forster. Lieut Loomis. 2Lt Ashley.
			CAPT LONGHURST (23RD NORTHD. FUS.) brought a party of 100 men to carry out the connection with troops on RIGHT. This was completed.	OFFICERS DIED OF WOUNDS—1 Lieut McIntosh
		11.20pm	The small force was relieved by the 58TH BDE and moved back to the rear.	OFFICERS MISSING BELIEVED KILLED – 1 2/Lt Trojan.
USNA - TARA LINE.	July 4th	8.50am	line. USNA – TARA Redoubts The Battalion proceeded to billets in MILLENCOURT	OFFICERS WOUNDED—10
MILLENCOURT	July 5th	4.0pm	The Battalion en-trused at MILLENCOURT marching on ALBERT and proceeded POMMIER	Capt Williams Lieut Bibby Lieut Atkinson 2Lt Purdy
POMMIER	July 6.	2.0am	Battalion in billets at POMMIER.	2Lt Mason 2Lt Robson
	"	8."	do.	2Lt Tugg
	9/11/".		A carrying party of 144 NCO's and men under 2 officers, supplies for carrying gas cylinders into the trenches in front of BIENVILLERS.	
	July 11th	1.0pm	Battalion remained in Billets at POMMIER.	
	July 12/13		The Battalion marched to billets at WARLINCOURT.	
WARLINCOURT.	July 13. 14.		The Battalion Remained in billets at WARLINCOURT.	
	July 15.	4.15pm	The Battalion marched to billets at LIGNEREUIL	

WAR DIARY or INTELLIGENCE SUMMARY.

BATTALION TYNESIDE SCOTTISH, (22nd (S) Bn. NORTHD. FUS.)

Army Form C. 2118.

SHEET 20.

Place	Date	Hour	Summary of Events and Information	Remarks and references to Appendices
LIGNEREUIL	July 15th	9 a.m.	The Battalion marched to billets at BAILLEUL-AUX-CORNAILLES.	
BAILLEUL-AUX-CORNAILLES	July 16th	9.30 a.m.	The Battalion marched to billets at DIVION	
DIVION	July 16/25		The Battalion remained in billets at DIVION. Steady training carried on daily. While at DIVION (July 22nd) the Army Commander inspected the troops and distributed the ribbons for the Honours and Awards to the following:- LIEUT. R.W. ROTHERFORD — MILITARY CROSS SERGT. J. MALCOME — MILITARY MEDAL CORP. I.T. KEMPSTER — Do. CORP. T.N. PATTERSON — Do. PTE. G. JOHNSON — Do.	2/Lt Petrie 2/Lt Ragrome 2/Lt Lambert 2/Lt Noonan Other Ranks Killed 15 Died of wounds 19 Missing believed Killed 4 Wounded 324 Missing 155
DIVION	July 26	12.51 p.m.	Owing to the weakness of the battalions, the battalion was amalgamated with the 23rd Northd. Fus: under the command of the O.C. 23rd Northd Fus and marched as one Battalion to billets at MAISNIL BOUCHE.	Total Casualties Officers 20 O.R. 517
MAISNIL BOUCHE	July 27th		The 4 companies (formed as 2 companies) took over the trenches in front of SOUCHEY under the command of O.C. 23rd Northd. Fus.	
	July 29th		Battalion Headquarters and details marched to VILLERS AU-BOIS to billets.	
VILLERS-AU-BOIS	July 27th–31st		The Companies remained in the trenches. Headquarters in billets at VILLERS-AU-BOIS.	

102nd Brigade.

ATTACHED 37th Division till 21.8.16.

34th Division from 22.8.16.

1/22nd BATTALION

NORTHUMBERLAND FUSILIERS

AUGUST 1 9 1 6 ::::

Volume VIII

WAR DIARY
OR
INTELLIGENCE SUMMARY.

(Erase heading not required.)

3rd BATTALION TYNESIDE SCOTTISH
(22nd (S) Bn. NORTHD. FUS.)
SHEET 21.

Army Form C. 2118.

Place	Date	Hour	Summary of Events and Information	Remarks and references to Appendices
VILLIERS-AU-BOIS.	August 1st	-	The Companies remained in the trenches and Battalion Headquarters at VILLIERS-AU-BOIS.	153 other ranks have already joined as reinforcements and the following officers:- 2nd Lt Faulder 2nd Lt Coates 2nd Lt Kirkup 2nd Lt Dawson-Scott 2nd Lt Calcium 2nd Lt Fenton 2nd Lt Stevens Casualties Killed 1 OR Wounded 10 - 2nd Lt TONHITLOCK joined 17/8/16
	August 2nd	-	The composite battalion on 22/23 Nov'rd. two was again formed into the two original battalions remaining in the trenches, the 22nd Battalion returned to billets in VILLIERS-AU-BOIS.	
	August 3rd/4 August 5/6/7/8/9/10/11/12/13 August 14/15 August 16/17/18/19/20/21 August 22		The Battalion remained in billets in VILLIERS-AU-BOIS. Training, Regrouping and Reorganising continued daily the Battalion took over trenches at SOUCHEZ On being relieved by Suffolk Rifles, Battalion marched to billets at ESTREE CAUCHIEZ. Refitting and training at ESTREE CAUCHIEZ. The Battalion rejoined 34th Division and marched to CALONNE-RICOURT, entraining here and detraining at LA GORGUE. From here by lorries to ERQUINGHEM at 11 am and detraining at 7.30 p.m. marched to billets in BOIS GRENIER line taking over SUBSIDIARY LINE of B sector.	Casualties Killed 2 OR Wounded 2 OR Lt Wetherington wounded 18/8/16 returned 23rd 30/8/16
	August 23			
	August 24	4.6 & 30 p.m.	Battalion H.Q. Reserve shelled, one direct hit on officers mess burying for ex-Capt. E. Roscoe, on being dug out 2nd/Lt T.O. WHITLOCK was found to be dead at of CAPT. E. ROSCOE, LIEUT. S. BRYSON. R.A.M.C. and 2nd LT. J.A. FAULDER assumed.	
	31		Battalion took over from two trenches B1. SubSector BOIS GRENIER line.	

Ken Benton
Commanding 3rd BATTALION TYNESIDE SCOTTISH,
(22nd (S) Bn. NORTHD. FUS.)

WAR DIARY
or
INTELLIGENCE SUMMARY.
(Erase heading not required.)

Army Form C. 2118.

3rd BATTALION TYNESIDE SCOTTISH
(22nd (S) Bn. NORTHD. FUS.)

Place	Date	Hour	Summary of Events and Information	Remarks and references to Appendices
BOIS GRENIER LINE	Sept 1st	—	The Battalion remained in the front line trenches.	Lieut WATTS 2/Lt TAYLOR wound SICK and CAPT RIDLEY's gunshot wound evacuated
	2/9/16 3/9 6/9 7/9 9/16 12		On being relieved by 21st North'd Fus, Battalion marched to billets in RUE MARLE. Refitting and training at RUE MARLE.	2/Lt MAFFERTY killed 11/9/16 2/Lt STODART wounded SICK
	9/9 15/9		"B" and "D" Coys relieved the company of the 23rd North'd Fus occupying KIBLE POST, remainder of battalion and headquarters being still at RUE MARLE. Capt WAUGH and a party of 150 men training in contemplation of a raid. Capt WAUGH led a raiding party at LA HOUSSOIE, after preliminary artillery bombardment. The enemy put up a barrage on his own front line, as though the raiding party reaches the enemy's wire & some reached his parapet. The casualties were 2 other ranks killed, 9 wounded, no identification was secured. Lt ROBSON at the same time led a small party of 30 men from the RUE DUBOIS SAILENT. The enemy expected the same manoeuvre at this point, and no identification was obtained.	2/Lt FENTON 5/9
	17/9		A further raid was attempted on the 17th, led by 2Lt BEGG and MACRAE, who had both been in the previous one. 2/Lt BEGG was wounded while advancing, and although the party reached the enemy wire, his identification who secured, the enemy again barraging his front line. 2/Lt BEGG was the only casualty. Batt'n relieves 21st N.F. and occupies front line, the 20th N.F. taking over KIBLE POST	Casualties wounded 2 OR 2/Lt HARDY SIMPSON BROUGGA joined 21 Sept
	21/9 22/9 25		Batt'n was relieved by 21st N.F. "A" Company took over KIBLE POST, "B" Company the subsidiary line astride DOGS LEG ROAD, and "C" Company the subsidiary line "C" line. "D" Company and headquarters returned to RUE MARLE. On the 26th "C" Company was relieved by the 19th N.F. and returned to RUE MARLE.	
	26 30th		Battalion remained as at 1st Sept.	

A.D.S.S./Forms/C. 2118.

Volume 10.
Army Form C. 2118.

WAR DIARY
or
INTELLIGENCE SUMMARY.

22nd Bn. North'd Fus. (3rd Tyneside Scottish)

SHEET No 23

(Erase heading not required.)

Instructions regarding War Diaries and Intelligence Summaries are contained in F.S. Regs., Part II. and the Staff Manual respectively. Title pages will be prepared in manuscript.

Place	Date	Hour	Summary of Events and Information	Remarks and references to Appendices
BOIS GRENIER LINE	Oct 10th		Bn relieved 21st N.F. in B.I. subsector.	Casualties 1 O.R. killed 3 O.R. wounded (1 accident)
	Oct 14th	0.15 A.M.	Bn was relieved by 21st N.F. and returned to billets in RUE MARLE.	
	Oct 15th		Bn relieved 21st N.F. in B.I. subsector	Casualties 1 O.R. wounded (at ent'g) 2nd Lt J. Glencross & 2nd Lt A. Park & C. Pippin wounded 16.10.16. 2nd Lt H. Skene evac. England sick 11.10.16. Casualties 1 O.R. wounded 2 Lt C.R. Gopsill joined 28th O.C.
	Oct 22nd		Bn was relieved by 21st N.F. and in turn relieved the 20th N.F. holding the following positions. "A" Coy – LILLE POST; half "B" Coy – Orchard; "C" Coy – RUE FLEURIE – LA VESEE branch; half "B" Coy – Subsidiary line. D Coy Subsidiary line between WINE and COWGATE Avenues	
	Oct 28th		Bn relieved 21st N.F. in B.I. subsector.	
	Oct 29th 30th 31st		Bn remained in front line trenches.	

Spencer Acklom Lt Col.
C'manding 3rd BATTALION TYNESIDE SCOTTISH,
(22nd (S) Bn. NORTH'D. FUS.)

22 NF Vol. No. 11. Sheet No 24

WAR DIARY
INTELLIGENCE SUMMARY.

Army Form C. 2118.

Place	Date	Hour	Summary of Events and Information	Remarks and references to Appendices
BOIS GRENIER LINE	1 Nov		Bn was relieved by 21st N.F. and moved to billets in RUE MARLE.	
	6 Nov		Bn relieves 21st N.F. in B1 Subsector.	
	7 Nov		A raid was carried out by a party of 22nd N.F. led by 2/Lt Pigarome. The wire was partly entered the enemy trenches and brought back identification. No casualties were incurred.	
	11 Nov		Bn was relieved by 21st N.F. and took up positions as follows:— "A" Coy – 2 platoons in ORCHARD POST, 2 platoons in SUBSIDIARY LINE; "B" Coy – SUBSIDIARY LINE; "C" Coy – LILLE POST; "D" Coy – RUE FLEURIE – LA-VESEE line.	Casualties 2/Lt wounded 2/Lt F. GLENRIN joined 17.11.16
	16 Nov		Bn relieves 21st N.F. in B1 Subsector.	
	21 Nov		Bn was relieved by 21st N.F. and moved to billets in RUE MARLE.	
	26 Nov		Bn relieves 21st N.F. in B1 Subsector.	
	28/30 Nov		Bn. remained in front line trenches.	

Spencer Newborn
Lt-Col.
Commanding 3rd BATTALION TYNESIDE SCOTTISH,
(22nd (S) Bn. NORTHD. FUS.)

9a

Vol 12

War Diary
Dec 1916

22nd (S) Bn Northd. Fus
(3rd Tyneside Scottish)

Army Form C. 2118.

WAR DIARY 3rd BATTALION TYNESIDE SCOTTISH,
(22nd (S) Bn. NORTHD FUS.)

or

INTELLIGENCE SUMMARY.

(Erase heading not required.)

Vol. No. 12.
SHEET No. 25.

Place	Date	Hour	Summary of Events and Information	Remarks and references to Appendices
BOIS GRENIER LINE	1st DEC		Batt was relieved by 21st N.F., and took up positions as follows:— A. Coy.: RUE FLEURIE B. Coy.: ORCHARD POST (2 platoons) SUBSIDIARY LINE (2 platoons) C. Coy.: SUBSIDIARY LINE D. Coy.: LILLE POST.	Lt. T.H. SKENE joined 7.12.16 as Transport Officer. Admitted hosp. sick 11.12.16.
	6 DEC		Batt relieved 21st N.F. in B1. Sub-sector.	
	11 DEC		Batt was relieved by 25th N.F. and then went into Divisional Reserve, being in billets and huts at ERQUINGHEM. Working parties and training.	Casualties Killed - 3 O.R. W'd. - 7 O.R.
	23 DEC		Batt moved into billets at RUE MARLE.	
	27 DEC		Batt relieved 21st N.F. in B1. Sub-sector.	
	31 DEC		Batt was relieved by 21st N.F., and took up positions as follows:— A. Coy.: ORCHARD POST (2 platoons) SUBSIDIARY LINE (2 platoons) B. Coy.: RUE FLEURIE C. Coy.: LILLE POST D. Coy.: SUBSIDIARY LINE	

WAR DIARY
or
INTELLIGENCE SUMMARY.

Army Form C. 2118.

22 N. Fus
SHEET No 26

Place	Date 1917	Hour	Summary of Events and Information	Remarks and references to Appendices
BOIS GRENIER LINE	1 Jany		Battalion remained in defensive posts in Subsidiary Line.	Casualties Killed 1 O.R.
	4 Jany		Battn relieved 21st N.F. in B1. Subs. sector.	Wounded 3. O.R.
	8 Jany		Battn, on being relieved by 21st N.F., moved into billets at RUE MARLE	1. O.R. killed on working party.
	12 Jany		Battn relieved 21st N.F. in B1. Subs. sector.	Draft of 200 O.R. Joined 7.1.17
ERQUINGHEM.	15 Jany		Battn. was relieved by 27th N.F. and moved with 102nd Bde. into Divisional Reserve. In huts at RUE DORMOIRE, ERQUINGHEM. Training and working parties.	Continued 2/Lt A.H.SMITH re-joined 4/17 Training Draft of 41 O.R. Joined 25.1.17
GODEWAERSVELDE	26 Jany 26 th - 31 Jany		Battn proceeded to GODEWAERSVELDE by bus. Training carried out.	

Spencer Newton
Comdg 3rd BATTALION TYNESIDE SCOTTISH
(22nd (S) Bn. NORTHD. FUS.)

WAR DIARY
OF
22nd (S) Bn. Northd. Fusiliers
(3rd TYNESIDE SCOTTISH)

MONTH --- FEBRUARY, 1917.

22(S) Bn NF
Volume 15
Sheet no 28. 22(S) Bn NF

WAR DIARY
or
INTELLIGENCE SUMMARY.
(Erase heading not required.)

Army Form C. 2118.

Instructions regarding War Diaries and Intelligence Summaries are contained in F.S. Regs., Part II. and the Staff Manual respectively. Title pages will be prepared in manuscript.

Place	Date 1917	Hour	Summary of Events and Information	Remarks and references to Appendices
ARRAS	13 May		Battalion on being relieved by 23rd N.F. went over break — 2 Companies in ARRAS and 2 Companies in ST NICHOLAS.	
	2nd to 7th May		Battalion employed on working parties in trenches.	
	7th to 8th May		Battalion marched to Redoubts at ECOIVRES	
	8th to 9th May		Battalion employed in suspension for MAGNICOURT for training	
	9th to 16th		Battalion underwent a training (See attached practice diary). Orderly mis the balance of the Brigade. The men showed intelligence and soon got a grip of the scheme in spite of numerous alterations & amendments. The Black, Blue and Alban lines were invariably captured.	
	12 May		Brigade paraded to witness presentation of award to officers and men of the Brigade by the Corps Commander. Sir Charles Kavanagh MC, MVO, DSO who expressed his pleasure in having the 34th Division under his command.	
	21st May		Battalion marched C X RUE ECOIVRES	
	22 May		Working parties supplied and platoon training carried on	
	23 May		Marched into PULINAIN relieving 10 Lincolns in Sector occupied previously. Bn at Coy under orders of 101st Brigade.	

WAR DIARY
or
INTELLIGENCE SUMMARY.
(Erase heading not required.)

Army Form C. 2118.

Volume 1st
Sheet No 29

Place	Date	Hour	Summary of Events and Information	Remarks and references to Appendices
ROCLINCOURT	Mar 28 to Mar 29		Battalion in the line. Our artillery fire very heavy. Enemy gave enfilade cutting wire of enemy 2 hrs 3rd line. Enemy fire scarce at times & an intense bombardment. mainly on communication trenches. Telephone wires cut at many places. Scaling Ladders placed in front line. Relieved by 23rd N.F. and took over their billets in ARRAS. Battalion Less working parties moved back to 'X' huts on being relieved by 20th N.F.	Casualties dining room Killed 4 Wounded 15 Capt 40 OR joined 16/3/17 2 Lts A.D. Gibson joined 21/3/17 2 Lt W.H. Templeton joined 25/2/17
	Mar 29 Mar 31			

Condry.
3rd BATTALION TYNESIDE SCOTTISH,
(22nd (S) Bn. NORTHD. FUS.)

13a 34 DIV

Vol/16

(6202) W 11186/M1151 350,000 12/16 McA. & W., Ltd. (Est. 781) Forms/W 3091/3. Army Form W. 3091.

Cover for Documents. ORIGINAL

Nature of Enclosures. Box 2252

WAR DIARY.

APRIL 1917.

22ND N.F. (3RD TYNESIDE SCOTTISH.)
Northumberland Fus
102. INF Bde

Notes, or Letters written.

WAR DIARY
or
INTELLIGENCE SUMMARY.
(Erase heading not required.)

Army Form C. 2118.

Volume 16
Sheet No 30

Place	Date	Hour	Summary of Events and Information	Remarks and references to Appendices
"X" Huts ECOIVRES ARRAS	1/3 Apl 4 Apl 8 Apl		Battalion remained at "X" Huts providing working parties. Battalion moved to ARRAS.	Drafts 49 ORs joined 1-4-17 2/Lt Bgrts killed 3-4-17 2/Lt L. Bushnell joined 7-4-17 2/Lt R. Barkway joined 7-4-17
	9 Apl	5:30 am	Battalion moved from ARRAS and took up its position in assembly trenches, A & B Coys in front line, C Coy in NEW STREET and D Coy in SPOON STREET. Battalion attacked. Resistance of enemy front line was overcome and advance pressed smartly to the 1st enemy trench (BLACK LINE). The artillery barrage front was not effective. Every manoeuvre & full advantage of ? by his snipers. Capt. L. Carter opened BLUE LINE opened.	4 ORs 7 ORs ? 7-4-17
		8:30 am	Ranking of his reserves and untimely arrival in the history of the line. The attack on the BROWN LINE was commenced by the 20th and 23 Bn N.F. preceeded by the 22 N.F. as Brigade Reserve. 22 Bn had very heavy losses. The 20 & 23 N.F. pushing on to the GREEN LINE and carrying a balloon in the Eastern outskirts of the BROWN LINE. 22 N.F. occupied the broken ground of the BROWN LINE. 21 N.F. the BLUE LINE 20, 10, 21 Brigades, reed in Cops 20 22 N.F. the 21 N.F. the 103 Brigade had failed to come up on Coys 20 later but the 103 Brigade had failed to come up on our right and left flank enfiladed leaving the flank enfiladed.	Lts/Sjt Ridley Wpld Batt Wpld/Sjt Watson Wpld/Cpl Maxwell-Leal W. Andrews ? Wpld/Cpl ? ? Wpld/Sjt Ellis Wpld/Sjt Wounded 9-4-17
		10 pm	Message received from Brigade H.Q. that 103rd Bgde were now noticed by 21st N.F. and 51st Division would move forward from the BLUE LINE and on the Lothern from 51st Division moved forward from the BLUE LINE. 22 N.F. were ordered to occupy the GAVRELLER WEG (the BROWN LINE to K of Railway).	
	10 Apl	6 am	The BROWN LINE was clear and took over the duty ? ? Snow had fallen during night making lines very uncomfortable. Later conditions were frost and then during the day.	

WAR DIARY or INTELLIGENCE SUMMARY

Army Form C. 2113.

Volume 16
March Ap 31

Place	Date	Hour	Summary of Events and Information	Remarks and references to Appendices
In field ARRAS	10 Apl	5 pm	F.O.O. reported enemy massing near GAVRELLE. 2 companies & machine guns sent to confirm this.	
		9.30 pm	Message from Brigade stated 12th & 4th Division were urgently to be being heavily attacked. Battalion were ordered to man the WESTERN BROWN LINE on both sides of the GAVRELLE HIGH ROAD.	
		11 pm	The ration entrainment from the front line at once and take up a position along this line. The men were moved at once to this position about 200 yards in for the night. The condition were miserable.	
	11 Apl	9 am	Battalion were ordered to a position to the sides of the SUNKEN road. 9 Pl & HQ and the SUNKEN road were occupied and by companies at intervals and completed by 2.30pm a plentiful supply of water was obtained. Troops would have handed over of future front line movement in Supp. and accumulation were done but as many men as possible were out in the available dug-outs and sleeps to sleep.	
		2.30 pm	Battalion warned by confidential orders to relieve 21st N.F. in BROWN LINE. A v.B of & E information was received regarding the position at ... the sector held. 2nd Lt SIMSON and Capt. CRANLEY were ordered to find out the position and report back any ... from the infantry that and any report that every near likely the confidence the battalion is now ...	
	12 Apl	8 am	This report has to be at this point to this mark. But up at N.C.O. and 4 men ... N.C.O. and 4 men are obviously inadequate number.	

WAR DIARY
or
INTELLIGENCE SUMMARY.

Army Form C. 2118.

Volume 16
Sheet no 32

Place	Date	Hour	Summary of Events and Information	Remarks and references to Appendices
In the field ARRAS	12 Apr	12 pm	The troops arranged for a Stokes howitzer barrage on the front, and for the flares to be arched when the troops left. The Stokes gun failed & the fire however and the attempt was postponed until later.	
	13 Apr	1 am	Enemy Singoon and fairly new presented along the trench recently to the front. They were challenged by two of the enemy who got on the parapet and fired at him and had thrown bombs. Lieut Simmons returned firing & woke the troops his men under and bombed the enemy whereupon much and occupying the position. A faint war cost to die not be of breeding formed and at dawn they can a faint of the enemy (evidently those who had been sniping and under a volley across the open rear when he last been sniping and under a volley across the open when he shot he was shot dead so to be "Sentries" but at 2nd Sentries but on trench BAILLEUL. The front was blocked. On discovery this arms or support at an lists revealed by law.	
		2.30 am	Some troops from the 103rd Brigade were sent up and replaced in the rear hand of the BROWN LINE & [?] troops were made on the railway cutting half way between G.S.O./34th Shewan. reached HQ of a Coy of front of [?] Col Chewan, G.S.O./34th Brigade. He stated that they were never seriously attacked, but tpth 101 & 102 Brigade. He stated that they were never seriously attacked, but attacks that were more much an intensity of the other battalion. Ignorance of the fact that units were not established to by the approach of the enemy due to have confusion in Oct.	
		4 am	Other information received that the Battalion would be relieved in the 142nd Brigade and moved by tom. The number of other ranks on the trenches at Nightfall was 300 in GREEN LINE 140 in Eastern BROWN LINE and 50 in BROWN Q.	

WAR DIARY
INTELLIGENCE SUMMARY
(Erase heading not required.)

Army Form C. 2118.

Volume 6
Sheet no 33

Place	Date	Hour	Summary of Events and Information	Remarks and references to Appendices
In the field ARRAS	13 April	6 pm	Orders having received that the 2nd Division on our left were pushing out patrols and that we were to conform an arrangement was made with the 10th K.R.R. that patrols should start at 6 pm. 2 Lieut Hardy and 2 Lieut Lang accompanied by a wireless with telephone and a meat some dog had at 2 Lt Douglas Coy arrived slowly to replace Hammond and followed him. My patrols beyond at dawn. See patrols the GREEN LINE and having the telephone line H.C. Summons N.Q Deft patrol that 2nd Summons patrol did penetrate through BELLEVE & had moved up and reported as far as normal from H.& G.B.S. C into an attack. See patrol penetrated as far as CAPT Bigly southern edge of BAILLEUL and were there ordered to dig in and took up Chemy pow and to form our outpost line in this normal. Ski remainder of the Company was ordered to B.C. ordered the EASTERN BROWN LINE to B Coy who would be occupy the GREEN LINE and A Coy who would be ordered to not to the WESTERN BROWN LINE. BLUE LINE to remain ordered as placed in the WESTERN BROWN LINE. A patrol was sent out towards GAVRELLE to look in touch with neutral in front of	
	14 April		2nd Summons on our left. See patrol was fired on from houses in my part. 9.-GAVRELLE and had great difficulty in advancing on any task. Advance party of the Grenadiers who were to relieve us arrived	2/Lt. A.W.A. Harris joined 10-4-17. Lt.Col. C. J. Eastland & Philip Atherton joined 22-4-17 Drafts 21.4/5 joined 22-4-17
		1.30 pm	4 Bedfords arrived - relief was commenced at	
		8 pm	Battn arrived at ARRAS and was accommodated in the Cavalry Barracks	
		10 pm	a movement was ready on their arrival	
MONCHY BRETON	15 April	3 am	Battn marched by bus to MONCHY BRETON	
		3.30 pm	Battalion in training	
	21 April		A Welsh investiture of Bgnrs ACQ	
	23 April 4 am		Battalion moved of at 3 am en route to ARRAS, marched in bus/scrub duties	

WAR DIARY
or
INTELLIGENCE SUMMARY.
(Erase heading not required.)

Army Form C. 2118.

Volume 16
Sheet No 34

Place	Date	Hour	Summary of Events and Information	Remarks and references to Appendices
ARRAS	23 Apl	7:55 pm	Orders received to march to neighbourhood of ST LAURENT BLANGY at 8.30 pm and occupy original front line Beluow Tunnel. Bn supplied to find but available cover was found for its men. Battalion assumed stations.	
	24 Apl		Occasional shelling but no casualties.	
	25 Apl		Bn was confirmed at H.Q of 23rd N.F. that they would relieve our up to the OPPY LINE north of FAMPOUX X road	
	26 Apl			
	27 Apl		2nd company sent 3 representatives each company to the OPPY LINE and leave forward to the line held by present position. It became notice from an advance of troops of 103rd Bde. Operation order received at about that the Brigade was to assemble in OPPY LINE at 2am and that the Brigade 26th N.F. would be wiped off an attack would be made on our front early tomorrow morning	
	28 Apl	2 am	Battalion moved into position in PUDDING TRENCH by 2 am	
		4.25 am	attack commenced. No information obtained except little C.4.5 from which the Brigade came up and informed us that the Brigade would probably be ordered to withdraw early in the morning. Dr Reid became clear and sure the attack had failed. But the situation was obscure. Lea Coy and their reserve came with definite instruction from the Division.	Capt J H Pitton Wounded 28.4.17 Wounded 28.4.17 Missing 19 1/2 Killed
		6.45 pm		
		8.50 pm	See objective of the attack was from the angle of CORONA TRENCH alm - I.14.c.1.9 to a point on the railway 100 yds east of its junction with the tunnel at I.13.6.10.55	

WAR DIARY
or
INTELLIGENCE SUMMARY.
(Erase heading not required.)

Army Form C. 2118.

Volume 16
Sheet No 35

Place	Date	Hour	Summary of Events and Information	Remarks and references to Appendices
In the field ARRAS	28/4/17		2a 23rd N.F. were to attack on the night of the 22nd N.F. on the left, the railway being the dividing line between battalions. — Zero to be 3 am. 2 Lt 22nd N.F. sent to meet us off at 10 pm to their position of assembly in CANDOR. The accurate details of the aviating situation being available the CO and adjutant remained at Brigade H.Q. till after midnight in order to receive any additional information which might come to hand. Guide 2/Lt 23rd N.F. told battalion to the strong assembly points in CANDOR FRENCH trench, has found confusion were men were in great difficulties, left across country the trenches being blocked by parties of 103rd & 104th Bde. N.Q. Ot Appears impossible to get any useful information from Bde. Adv. N.Q. The CO's information then in CALABAR FRENCH was occupied by their brigade which a guide who stated the not being ready when the enemy aid it.	
	29/4/17	1.15 am	C.O. started with adjutant for a point B on the night of the attack — 5 company to push off from Bath / CALABAR and with one platoon detailed to mop up about race in CANDOR. Company formed in support whilst a company was putting up flares continuously as a screen. The enemy who were firing the 4/N were dead a distance 100 yards a much galled rom known, severe Co bright spent rifle & machine gun fire along the line of CALABAR. They were driven back and the advance was continued till the forms of confusion are found to be from all	
	3 am		Being mopped by paying fire from motor were from N, E + S.	

WAR DIARY
INTELLIGENCE SUMMARY

Army Form C. 2118.

Volume 16
Sheet no 36

Place	Date	Hour	Summary of Events and Information	Remarks and references to Appendices
Sulzbach ARRAS 2	29/4	3.20 am	The advance of the machine gun fire from the SOUTH slowed but the 23rd N.F. had made its proper pace. B Company therefore occupied & consolidated the NORTHERN portion of CALABAR which was the only available cover from fire and the remainder of the attacking company's withdrew to CAM TRENCH and to CANDOR. A small party of men moved into Lt. ROBSON and 2nd Lt. SIMSON remained in the direction of trench about 80 yards EAST of CALABAR where they were completely isolated. So the machine guns & message timed 2.50 am was received by O.C. 23rd N.F. at 3.20 am stating that any further resistance is impossible. It appeared unlikely that the 23rd N.F. could be at the position if necessary by 3am and that the attack should therefore be postponed. It was 1450 note to completely with have instructions and orders was informed accordingly and a full report of the situation made to there. Shown were also taken to the 22nd N.F. of the situation in definition but may not been received. Our casualties asking for their definitions but had not yet been received. Our casualties in the attack were 50 - a remarkable small total, partly due to the foot that the formation of the ground caused the enemy's machine gun fire to pass over the men's heads during the first 200 yards of the advance which then ch.. opened passage fell behind. A Artillery under the 2/off REA successful in breaking up an enemy working from and rendering the enemy where they pal into touch with 23rd N.F. about IBC no 551	

Army Form C. 2118.

WAR DIARY
or
INTELLIGENCE SUMMARY.
(Erase heading not required.)

Volume 16
Book no 37

Instructions regarding War Diaries and Intelligence Summaries are contained in F.S. Regs., Part II. and the Staff Manual respectively. Title pages will be prepared in manuscript.

Place	Date	Hour	Summary of Events and Information	Remarks and references to Appendices
In the field ARRAS	29 April	8.30 pm	Meanwhile 2/Lt ROBSON's patrol had been attacked by 30 or 40 of the enemy who tried to make him & his division M coult repel fire & bombs. A runner from 2/Lt Robson reached Batt. H.Q. and another had a 2nd Lt TAYLOR and a small patrol who carried orders for 2/Lt Robson to withdraw. As the failure moved out the enemy opened a heavy barrage and shot. 2/Lt Robson was fatally wounded in the jaw. Cpl [?] was fatally wounded in the leg. 2/Lt Robson & party had the patrol successful in today. Seeing the enemy are continued to fall back without casualties. Patrols were pushed out and established in small posts will be in consolidate. Our positions at I.13.a.2.1.	
	29/30	1 am	In the enemy sap a few stragglers cut in two smile pasts at I.13.c.4.6 and I.13.c.5.8. respectively were consolidated	
	30 April May 2	2am	Relief of Battalion by 2nd Bedfordshire Fusiliers was completed and we marched to billets near BLANGY.	

[signature] Mackenzie
Major
Commanding 3rd BATTALION TYNESIDE SCOTTISH,
(22nd (S) Bn. NORTHD. FUS.)

WAR DIARY or INTELLIGENCE SUMMARY.

Army Form C. 2118.

Vol 17

Place	Date	Hour	Summary of Events and Information	Remarks and references to Appendices
ARRAS	2 Aug 17	12.30 pm	Battalion entrained for HAUTVILLE.	
HAUTVILLE	3/6 Aug		Battalion training.	
SUS ST LEGER 7 Aug			Battalion marched to SUS ST LEGER	
NEUVILLETTE 8 Aug			Battalion marched to NEUVILLETTE	
FIENVILLERS 9 Aug			Battalion marched to FIENVILLERS	
	9 Aug to 2 Aug		Battalion in training. Platoon fire slow musketry come — snapping appendix dupes - snapshooting - 5 rounds & min. Spare likelier firing to fire man with bar rapidity, fire discipline, use of ground, cover & formation. 2 i/c man initiated in all weapons if fields of fire — rifle grenade, Lewis gun & bombs. Simple attack practices carried out. Clothing & equipment been in good condition.	
CANDAS			Entrained for ARRAS	
ST NICHOLAS	30 Aug 31 Aug		Arrived ARRAS and marched to ST NICHOLAS	

General Watson
Lt Col
Cdg. 3rd BATTALION TYNESIDE SCOTTISH,
(22nd (S) Bn. NORTHD. FUS.)

WAR DIARY
or
INTELLIGENCE SUMMARY.
(Erase heading not required.)

Army Form C. 2118.

2/2 W. N. F. 18
Sheet No 38

Place	Date	Hour	Summary of Events and Information	Remarks and references to Appendices
ST. NICHOLAS (ARRAS)	1st 2nd 3rd and 4th June	8 pm	Battalion in Bivouacs. Battalion moved off to relieve South of GAVRELLE and occupied Battle position for advance on GREENLAND HILL Scale – jar was arranged in the way but no casualties were suffered	
WESTERN edge of GREENLAND HILL	5 June	7.30 p.m	Battalion formed up in assembly trenches according to programme with 21st N.F. on Right and 20th N.F. on Left and ½ of the 26th N.F. in Rear. The objective of 102nd Brigade was the capturing & consolidating as a main line trenches the enemy trenches CHARLIE and CURTH and the consolidating of a line & strong points on the farside of CUTHBERT and COD Walks. Zero was 8 pm.	Casualties to 22/6/17 Killed 2/Lt W.K. Simson Capt T.H. Waugh 8 O.R. Died of Wds 6 O.R. Wounded 174 O.R. Lt. Lees ((Rev)) 2/Lt. A.V. D. Murie Missing 80 O.R. 2/Lt. H. McDonald (Believed killed)
		7.58 p.m	The enemy opened a barrage on CHIPS and our front line inflicting several casualties including a sergeant commanding a Lewis gun platoon. The barrage lasted 1 minute. The enemy opened on the left company with field guns heavily after zero but casualties were not heavy for the front so good & the advance from zero was pushed in musical order.	
		Zero 8 pm	The flank companies were held, previous levels the advance left the station culminated with the capture & the tranch numbered b and from the Junction of CHARLIE and CUTHBERT was practically wiped out by fire from WIT Wood. 25 officers and 2 men were left only over Left wind &	

WAR DIARY
or
INTELLIGENCE SUMMARY.
(Erase heading not required.)

Army Form C. 2118.

Volume 18
Sheet No 39.

Place	Date	Hour	Summary of Events and Information	Remarks and references to Appendices
GREENLAND HILL	5th June		The situation was somewhat critical under line of CHARLIE had been abandoned by our team owing to the advance of By rifle grenades. Any station tapping occurred during our entry into CHARLIE where our second armed fell noticed supports of the enemy in bomb distance and anticipated. Our rifle coys, my Road 1/6 down carbine length of trench by bombing before they found a road mile too much in rear feared. The left company also bombed entrance and became the trench about 30 yards NE of the junction of CHARLIE with CUTHBERT. Meanwhile our platoon detailed to occupy CUTHBERT had advanced and taken possession. That trench where the drop of support and consolidating work was immediately commenced. Complete and	
		11 am	platoon were quickly reorganized and the right renewed to A.W.R. H.Q. About 11am the enemy make the first apparent attempt to molest us holding up towards us from Osiris. The evening being fine, given by the advance heavily that no great difficulty was experienced in repulsing him by a barrage of rifle grenades. Any further most wandering or entry into the unoccupied to enemy lead to another strafe.	
		12pm	By midnight the consolidation of our position was well advanced so far as digging is concerned.	

WAR DIARY or INTELLIGENCE SUMMARY.

Army Form C. 2118.

Volume 18
Sheet No 40.

Place	Date	Hour	Summary of Events and Information	Remarks and references to Appendices
GREENLAND HILL	5/6 June	12 midnight	The posts in CUTHBERT were in occupation of their position. The left of the posts having been supported with a specific view to sweeping our left flank with fire should need arise.	
	6 June	2 am	At 2 am, a party of the enemy were observed outside of the sunken road and advancing up the junction of CHARLIE and CUTHBERT. At the same time a barrage of trench mortar and rifle grenades was put down on the NORTHERN end CHARLIE. The enemy then made a very determined bombing attack on the trench junction and succeeded in advancing to within [?] of our driver of the junction of CHARLIE considerable casualties during this encounter. His force of the enemy must have been also heavy.	
	2.15 am	About 2.15 am a body of the enemy estimated at the strength of 1 Battalion was seen about the exit of WIT Trench and was aligned at the sunken road. They advanced across the open with their rifles slung and machine guns free from us fire in CUTHBERT and were immediately caught under our rifle and machine gun fire from our posts in CUTHBERT and from the trench junction of CHARLIE and CUTHBERT and were immediately under accurate rapid fire. The enemy apparently unable to advance continued in narrow formation. He was observed also running back in about equally narrow formation after apparently	
	2.15 am to 3.40 am		to within 250 yds of our position.	
	6 am		Rather smaller bodies of the men suffered severely from Lewis gun and rifle fire under difficult to detect any appreciable Grenade vs S.A.A. could have been collected.	

#353 Wt. W2544/1454 700,000 5/15 D. D. & L. A.D.S.S./Forms/C. 2118.

WAR DIARY or INTELLIGENCE SUMMARY

Army Form C. 2118. Volume 18. Sheet No 41.

Place	Date	Hour	Summary of Events and Information	Remarks and references to Appendices
GREENLAND HILL	6 Jun		The enemy made no further attempt to regain the ground lost and during the night full storm and heavy barrage action and commenced their withdrawal from advancing the communication trenches and carrying parties.	
	7 Jun	1.40 am	At 1.40 am I and the enemy suddenly opened an intense heavy barrage of trench mortars and rifle grenades upon the junction CHARLIE—CUTHBERT and enters a few minutes after fire. The Germans advanced in unexpected strong force. The enemy then attacked in a most determined manner along the whole of our frontage. The party made considerable progress during the temporary confusion which resulted from our counter and succeeded in reoccupying CHARLIE for about 50 yards and in CUTHBERT side to about half its full length in CUTHBERT on the centre part. The advance was however considerably interfered by the rifle grenade fire I sent the owner of the German at the CHARLIE—CUTHBERT trench junction. Later the enemy of Officers N.C.O's a party was injured in CHARLIE when 26 minutes later could attack. A rifle was even in reserve rifle grenades the party attacked the enemy across the top of the left unoccupied side and fired to their and was leaving the machine gun behind. At the same time a party from the German on all from retaking the attention in CUTHBERT. The work of 2/Lt A.W.D. MARK M.C on the action left was most excellent. He...	

WAR DIARY
or
INTELLIGENCE SUMMARY.
(Erase heading not required.)

Army Form C. 2118.

Volume 18
Sheet No 42.

Place	Date	Hour	Summary of Events and Information	Remarks and references to Appendices
GREENLAND HILL	7 June	12th night	No further advance. Enemy unfortunately occupied and the battalion was withdrawn to their support, relay base & bivouacs at ST NICHOLAS	
ST NICHOLAS	8/11 June		Battalion in working parties.	
RAILWAY CUTTING	11/14 June		Battalion in working parties.	
POINT DE JOUR				
GREENLAND HILL	14/17 July		Battalion relieved 20th N.F. in support of 11th Div. During the attack this battalion took part being in and in two distinct waves and in any event would never have been taken. The battalion was infused and one section had under the support of Tarveren. Battalion relieved by 20th N.F. and returned to back GRAILWAY CUTTINGS ST NICHOLAS	
RAILWAY CUTTING	17th July			
ST NICHOLAS	23 June		Battalion relieved by 7 Yorks. Bay. returned to bivouac	
ARRAS	27 June 11.26 am		Battalion entrained at ARRAS for BUNEVILLE.	
BUNEVILLE	27 June 4 pm		Battalion arrived at BUNEVILLE when training was carried out	
	3 June			

Spencer Acklom
Lt. Col.

Cdg 20 BATTALION TYNESIDE SCOTTISH,
(22nd (S) Bn. NORTHD. FUS.)

WAR DIARY
or
INTELLIGENCE SUMMARY.

(Erase heading not required.)

Army Form C. 2118.

Volume 19
Sheet 4, 3

Vol 19

Place	Date	Hour	Summary of Events and Information	Remarks and references to Appendices
BUNEVILLE	1/7/17		Battalion in Bivouac	
PERONNE	5 Jul	1 am	Battalion marched to TINCQUES and entrained for PERONNE.	2/Lt R W Watts reported 10-7-17 Draft J. 176 Killed 13-7-17
HERVILLY	8 Jul	3 pm	Battalion marched from PERONNE to HERVILLY. Guides reconnoitred enabling route/guides provided	
VILLERET	9 Jul	10.30 pm	Battalion took over trenches from 2nd LANCERS. One Raid by enemy	2/Lt A.H. Hudden arrived 25-7-17
		9 pm	On trenches. Enemy trench mortars active. Otherwise quiet	2/Lt I.W. Schitts 2/Lt I.M. Hitchman Arrived 27-7-17
	25/26		Battalion relieved by 13th Royal Scots and 10th Lincolns, Coy having relieved Nos. 1, 2, 3, 4 & Coys, and battalion Nos 6 & 7.	Casualties during march Wounded 10 (including 1 accidentally) Died of wds 1
BERNES	26/31		Battalion took over billets at BERNES.	
			Battalion in at BERNES as ordinary routine carried out. Training carried out.	

Spencer Acklom Lt. Col.
Commdg. 3rd BATTALION TYNESIDE SCOTTISH (22nd (S) Bn. NORTHD. FUS.)

WAR DIARY or INTELLIGENCE SUMMARY.

(Erase heading not required.)

Army Form C. 2118.

22 NF
VOLUME 20

August 1917

Place	Date	Hour	Summary of Events and Information	Remarks and references to Appendices
BERNES	1st		Warning order received from 102nd Bde. to the effect that the Battn. will take over A1 (VADENCOURT) Sub Sector from 26th NF tomorrow. — Reconnaissance to be carried out and 2 Officers and 20 O.R. to be sent to the line to go out with 26th NF patrols tonight. — 2/Lieuts DICKINSON and _____ detailed for this duty. —	
VADENCOURT	2nd		Report received that the 26th NF patrol to which 2/Lt DICKINSON and his 10 men were attached encountered a hostile patrol, quite unsupported through lack of proper covert protection. — Abrupt instructions were not given left, the patrol moved out with the result that a sentry group composed of 2 Officers and a NCO & 1 man of the 26th NF were fired upon by the main body of our patrol and Pt. _____ was wounded. The 26th NF 2/Lt. being killed. — These mixed patrols are highly unsatisfactory and the system of proper patrols of Officers and units goes in a proper patrol is altogether b.d. — The 102nd Bde. relieved the 103rd 18th this evening. The 22nd N.F. taking over A1 Subsector with their RIGHT upon the OMIGNON RIVER and their LEFT on RED WOOD. — Bdge. H.Q. at VADENCOURT. — FRENCH troops (118th Regiment) are on our RIGHT, and the 23rd N.F. in A2 on our LEFT. — 20th and 21st N.F. in Support & Reserve respectively. — The distribution of the Battn. is as follows. — 'B' Co. (Capt ALLAN) RIGHT — 'C' Co. (Capt HARDY) LEFT. — 'A' Co. (Capt ATKINSON) Support. Excepting 1 Platoon attached to 'C' Co. — ① A mixed patrol of 22nd & 26th NF is again going out tonight in accordance with instructions. —	2 O.R. wounded. ① per Sketch B/91 Defences.
	3rd		The mixed patrol reported to above was encountered by a hostile patrol in SOMERVILLE WOOD at 11.15 p.m. — The enemy were fired on, and whilst after returning the fire for a few moments. The enemy officers to patrol were most conspicuous in passing and keep their deposition close to them. Best was in general occasion recently. — NO MAN'S LAND	

WAR DIARY or INTELLIGENCE SUMMARY

Army Form C. 2118.

Sheet 45.

Place	Date	Hour	Summary of Events and Information	Remarks and references to Appendices
VADENCOURT	4th		is remarkably quiet in this sector and apart from plenty of sniping for consumption between small patrols. The chief feature between the lines is SOMERVILLE WOOD where we keep a standing patrol all day in order to forestall the enemy in that area. — (2)	(2) Patrol orders for night 3/4/17
	4th		One patrol under 2/Lt GORRILL which went out to FISHER CRATER last night fought a hostile party moving at a quick pace along the ridge NE of them about M 20 85 90. 2/Lieut GORRILL's patrol opened rapid fire and the enemy halted. Their strength is estimated at 50. It is thought that some were wounded as cries for assistance & groans were heard. There is very little artillery activity in this sector. A great deal of German correspondence is being received on the Fatigue of a nest of guns which the enemy is massing in this sector. A prisoner came down on our lines at 10.15 pm having lost German regiment.	
	5th		Last night the enemy shelled the disused trench in NO MANS LAND from which their patrol had been caught by the fire of 2/Lt GORRILL's platoon on the previous night. The enemy, however, when seen going out on patrol in the same area had chosen a different place to lie up and sustained no casualties. — 2/Lt STEPHENSON's patrol located an unoccupied enemy post 100 yds S. of DOGLEG WOOD. He on slightening was fired on from the direction of CRESSY TRENCH which will remain a remarkable improvement in the field of fire towards the Rivers — The Bay has been Quiet. ③	③ Patrol orders for night 5/6/17
	6th		2/Lt G.A. BROWN's patrol reconnoitred the FISHER CRATER area last night but saw no enemy. 2/Lt PEACOCK's patrol, after reviewing the dry patrol in SOMERVILLE WOOD examined various localities in the vicinity and collected useful information. Hostile artillery was very quiet during the day and enemy of our patrols saw but very few and KiD.	④ Patrol orders for night 6/7/17

Army Form C. 2118.

WAR DIARY
or
INTELLIGENCE SUMMARY.
(Erase heading not required.)

Sheet 46.

Instructions regarding War Diaries and Intelligence Summaries are contained in F.S. Regs., Part II. and the Staff Manual respectively. Title pages will be prepared in manuscript.

Place	Date	Hour	Summary of Events and Information	Remarks and references to Appendices
VADENCOURT	7th		The standing patrol of 2 sections under 2/Lt WRIGHT which remained in SOMERVILLE WOOD during daylight yesterday was encountered by two separate enemy patrols after dusk and before the arrival of our relieving patrol. — 2/Lt WRIGHT had posted out his advanced sentry posts and received due warning by the approach of the enemy searchers from the S.E. — The enemy patrol strength drawn 0.75 to 1.6 and rifle fire & were seen to carry away one of their number, whilst the casualties we inflicted — meanwhile a second party of the enemy had advanced against the wood from the N.E. and had been met by a standing patrol of 1 NCO & 2 men who drove them off. With N/23 rifle grenades. — 2/Lt STOBBS' platoon relieved 2/Lt WRIGHT and reconnoitred the MAX WOOD area, finding two dugouts about G.32.d. 70.02 and a short section of camouflaged trench. — No enemy were seen. nor did 2/Lt G.A.BROWN's platoon find any hostile parties See any hostile parties. — The enemy put down an artillery barrage on the W. portion of SOMERVILLE WOOD between 10.16 and 11.16 p.m. which was no doubt intended to assist their patrolling operations mentioned above and which belong to the first of 2/Lt STOBBS' platoon from our lines. — ⑤	2/Lt C.R. COOPER rejoined. 2. O.R. Wounded ⓐ Patrols out nightly 7/8 ⓑ Patrol 12a go 8/9
	8th		Our Day patrol took up its position in the dugouts at G.32.d. 70.00 & remained there gathering daylight ended ⓐ in SOMERVILLE WOOD. — The enemy has not been in NO MAN'S LAND since his encounter with 2/Lt WRIGHT's party. — The enemy shelled DRAGOON POST this morning + knocked in the entrance to a dugout. — He also shelled SOMERVILLE WOOD lightly. — ⑥	ⓒ Patrol 12a go 8/9

2353 Wt. W2544/1454 700,000 5/15 D.D. & L. A.D.S.S./Forms/C. 2118.

Army Form C. 2118.

WAR DIARY
or
INTELLIGENCE SUMMARY.
(Erase heading not required.)

Sheet 47

Instructions regarding War Diaries and Intelligence Summaries are contained in F. S. Regs., Part II. and the Staff Manual respectively. Title pages will be prepared in manuscript.

Place	Date	Hour	Summary of Events and Information	Remarks and references to Appendices
VADENCOURT	9th		Our standing patrol remained in SOMERVILLE WOOD. During daylight yesterday and to-day one man killed and another wounded by a shell. — Last night our patrol found a German Patrol in the wire near SOMERVILLE WOOD and a diary was found in the patrol. Within up to the 8th August proved that the snipers must have been killed or wounded in the patrol encounter of the 8th instant. — The man belongs to the 61st Infantry Regiment. — We have selected a sniper's nest post between LONE TREE POST and TUMULUS. — It is an excellent position and will greatly strengthen our defences of this portion of our line. — Lieut MAUGHAN carried out an excellent patrol last night through FISHER CRATER where he found the body of a German which had been evidently lying there for some months, but the shoulder strap of which proved an interesting identification. — Lieut MAUGHAN also examined the wire round ST HELENS trench & found a gap in the wire about M.3.&.7.6. — The Battalion is to be relieved by the 21st NF to-morrow night. —	Patrol encounter on night 7/8/16 (?)
	10th		2nd Lieut MAUGHAN again carried out a very satisfactory patrol, and entering and making a thorough examination of ST HELEN'S TRENCH which he found deserted and much dilapidated. — Under orders for the relief of the Battn by 21st NF are cancelled. — The 10th Div is to be relieved by the 103rd Bde to-night. —	1 OR Killed 1 OR Wounded

Army Form C. 2118.

WAR DIARY
or
INTELLIGENCE SUMMARY.
(Erase heading not required.)

Sheet 48.

Instructions regarding War Diaries and Intelligence Summaries are contained in F. S. Regs. Part II. and the Staff Manual respectively. Title pages will be prepared in manuscript.

Place	Date	Hour	Summary of Events and Information	Remarks and references to Appendices
BERNES VADENCOURT	11.		The Battn was relieved last night by the 26th N.F. and marched back to BERNES. Our patrols stayed out in NO MANS LAND till dawn but saw no sign of the enemy. — A Draft of 33 men joined the Battn this evening from the 103rd Brigade owing to the amalgamation of the 24th and 27th N.F. —	2/Lt C.S. ANDERSON 2/Lt M. BABBITT joined from 24/27 N.F
	12.		The Battn is now consists of 3 Companies only, D Co having been cut right away. Lieut. W BROWN — Each company is now organized in 3 platoons.	
	13.		The Brigade moved into the line again this evening, taking over B Sector from the 101st Bde. — The Battn relieved the 16th Royal Scots in support. Major Harris was appointed to superintend the 18th School at VRAIGNES from today, relieving Capt. CHARLTON who has rejoined for duty and is acting as Second in command — A Draft of 62 O.R. joined the B. today. —	
	14.		Battalion in intermediate line behind village, and finding working parties.	

#353 Wt. W2544/1454 700,000 5/15 D.D.&L. A.D.S.S./Forms/C. 2118.

WAR DIARY
or
INTELLIGENCE SUMMARY.
(Erase heading not required.)

Army Form C. 2118.

Sheet 49

Place	Date	Hour	Summary of Events and Information	Remarks and references to Appendices
VILLERET	15 16 17 18		Battalion still in INTERMEDIATE LINE behind VILLERET POSTS. On the 16th Battalion Headquarters moved to RUELLES WOOD. "C" Company under Capt. Allen Marr at this time engaged on special work in connection with the defence of VILLERET, under supervision of 207th Field Co. R.E. Work of previous specially complemented by G.O.C. 102nd Inf. Bde.	96.
HARGICOURT	19		Battalion moved into the HARGICOURT (LEFT SUB-SECTOR) taking over from 23rd North'd Fus. (4th Tyneside Scottish). Disposition:- B Coy. (Capt. Allen) RIGHT FRONT. A Coy. (Sec. Lieut. Cooper) LEFT FRONT. C Coy. Capt. Marr CLOSE SUPPORT. D Coy. (A/Capt. N. Brown) also in SUPPORT. Lieut. Col. Ackland proceeded on sick leave to England. Capt. Charlton took command of Battalion. Sec. Lieut. F.G. Moore and Lieut. W. Brown promoted to acting rank of CAPTAIN.	A/G.O. Lion to England sick. 96.
do.	20		Fairly quiet day on our front. North, which know very well now appears to be licking up. On our left in 35th Div. Front the two been a good deal of artillery + M. Gun activity consequent upon the attack by 35th Division on VILLEMONT FARM and the KNOLL and hostile counter attacks. Firing off during the day with heavy loss to the enemy.—(8) Patrol orders for 96.	(8) Patrol orders for 20/9/17

WAR DIARY
or
INTELLIGENCE SUMMARY.
(Erase heading not required.)

Army Form C. 2118.

Sheet 50

Place	Date	Hour	Summary of Events and Information	Remarks and references to Appendices
HARGICOURT	21		Fairly quiet day on Battalion front apart from small number of medium hostile trench mortars and grenades. Continued hostil artillery activity on our immediate left on 5th Divisional front. Enemy shelled GILLEMONT FARM heavily intermittently during the day. Hostile air-craft very active. Weather bright and good for observation. (9)	(9) Patrol orders attached.
	22		Normal quiet day. Hostile retaliation to our mine cutting and heavy trench mortar shoots weak. Enemy shelling slightly confined to our par lines and a certain amount of ammunition work. A fighting patrol under Sec. Lieut. Piegrome wounded. Hostile patrol in neighbourhood of Rifle at Trench F.30.3 (Ref. GILLEMONT FARM) which quickly retired towards their own lines on the approach of our patrol. Capt. A.T. MORGAN C.F. reported on the 19.8.17 to C/E Chaplain 22nd and 23rd N.F. and Gen. V.R. ROGERS to ENGLAND. (10)	(10) Patrol orders attached.
	23		Spasmodic artillery activity both our own and enemys. Marked increase	2 OR wounded

WAR DIARY
or
INTELLIGENCE SUMMARY

Army Form C. 2118. Sheet 51.

Place	Date	Hour	Summary of Events and Information	Remarks and references to Appendices
HERVILLY	25		in enemy's artillery retaliation both in counter-attack work and retribution. A tying patrol under Sec. Lieut. EDGELEY which left our lines at 10.30pm encountered hostile patrol near RIFLE PIT TRENCH. Our patrol brought fresh rifle & Lewis gun fire and enemy patrol quickly scattered, ran for their own lines. We had no casualties. Ground afterwards searched but no identifications @ secured. (1) Battalion relieved in LEFT SUBSECTOR by 23rd N.F. and one Company, 11th SUFFOLKS the relief taking over VALLEY & AUSSAH POSTS. Battalion in huts. "D" Company attached to 207th F.Coy. R.E. in connection with special work during forthcoming operations. On night of 28th Battalion moved forward to the AARGICOURT area arriving with orders of G.O.C. 101 Bde with the exception of "D" Company who we attached to 207th F.Coy. R.E. The work assigned to A. B & C. Companies is carrying R.E. material, ammunition etc. in the attack on COLOGNE RIDGE by 101 Inf Bde of 34th Division.	2nd Lt. LAING joined

WAR DIARY or INTELLIGENCE SUMMARY

Army Form C. 2118.

Sheet 52

Place	Date	Hour	Summary of Events and Information	Remarks and references to Appendices
AERILLY (Contd)	26		101 Bde attacked enemy trenches strike on the high ground known as COLOGNE RIDGE. The Stephin engaged by Wire buy S.F. trenches on a front of 2000 yards and to an average depth of 400 yards. The trenches being strike on high ground with Garrison commanding the HARGICOURT VALLEY running N.E. and the VILLERET VALLEY running S.E. of 22nd N.F. were detailed in company further supports transport as follows...	2/Lt A BRADNUM (Wounded (at duty)) 7 OR Killed 1 " Died of Wds 32 OR (wounded) 25 " Gassed 1 " Missing
HARGICOURT	26	4.30am	'A' Coy carry for 16th ROYAL SCOTS 'B' " " 10th LINCOLNS 'C' " " 11th SUFFOLKS 'D' " took under 207th Field Coy RE diggers	
			STRONG POINTS in the captured system out wiring in front of captured trenches. ZERO hour fixed for the attack 4.30am.	
		4.30am	Immediately the attack commenced our Coys, companies, which had during the night been standing to near their respective dumps in HARGICOURT, followed our NO MANS LAND in rear of the Battalions to whom mentioned to whom they were materiall that a copious supply of RE material continuation got forward to the new position, in spite of the fact that a heavy Artillery barrage was put down on NO MANS LAND	

WAR DIARY
or
INTELLIGENCE SUMMARY.

Sheet 13

Place	Date	Hour	Summary of Events and Information	Remarks and references to Appendices
			and on the original BRITISH FRONT line, the carriers did their job with remarkable coolness and gallantry, arriving at the objective and sometimes even before, within half an hour of the line attacking troops. Worked this point. Enemy shelling in the AARGICOURT area was severe throughout the whole of the day, enemy making free use of gas shells. "B" & "A" Coys. whose re-filling points were near THE EGG were instructed to create the area by 101 Rifle Staff on account of the concentrated enemy shelling in the locality. Casualties are fairly heavy in old Coys. "A" Coy. Hours carried with the exception of S.P.'s. The Civil Company advanced a STRONG POINT in captured system at F.30.c.85.00. other work could not be proceeded with during the hours of daylight in this neighbourhood. hostile M. Guns firing from direction of TRIANGLE TRENCH being specially active.	
AARGICOURT 24/h			Scavengers still in same position and engaged on work similar to 26th	

WAR DIARY
or
INTELLIGENCE SUMMARY.

(Erase heading not required.)

Army Form C. 2118.

3rd BATTALION TYNESIDE SCOTTISH,
(22nd (S) Bn. NORTHD. FUS.)

Sheet 54

Place	Date	Hour	Summary of Events and Information	Remarks and references to Appendices
ARGICOURT	27 (CONT'D)	—	From early morning of the 27th throughout the night rain fell incessant, accompanied by a strong wind. Trenches were soon in a deplorable condition in places almost waist deep in mud, and in every dugout, everyone tried hard to be dry out of its morass. In spite of arduous and wet conditions everyone was cheerful during the tour of duty. Men everywhere were soaked to the skin with no adequate shelter. Hostile shelling not quite so intense. Enemy M. Gun fire active, parties being specially exposed in No mans land.	
	28	—	Battalion relieved from support, special work which over R. INTERMEDIATE LINE, neighbourhood of COTE WOOD between 24/27th N.F. in this area.	
	29	—	Battalion still in same position and furnishing working & carrying parties do.	
	30	—	do	
	31	—	Battalion took over left sub-sector 102nd Bde front, relieving 2d NF.(1⁄8TS) A.D.T.C. Companies formed B Coy from in support 103 Bde (9th NF) on our left. 2nd NF.(2⁄4 TS) on our right flank. night of 31/1 Sept	

PATROL SCHEME

for the NIGHT 3rd/4th August.

(A). Patrol consisting of 1 complete Platoon of "A" Company with an additional Lewis Gun attached.
The patrol will take up a position in SOMERVILLE WOOD at 10.30 p.m. near its EASTERN CORNER, and will throw out three standing patrols of 2 men to the N, E, and S. to give warning of the enemy's approach. These three standing patrols will be connected to their main body by string.
The patrol will attack any hostile party which is seen in the neighbourhood. It will not, however, move E. of a line drawn due S.W. from the E. Corner of SOMERVILLE WOOD.

(B). Patrol consisting of one complete platoon of "B" Company with an additional Lewis Gun attached.
The Patrol will move out from our Lines at 10.15 p.m. by the road from CRESSY TRENCH to FISHER CRATER - Turning NORTHWARDS near the Road Junction G.2.d.32.55. They will move up the valley towards MAX WOOD and will take up a position from which they can observe the ground between MAX and SOMERVILLE WOODS, the former of which will be reconnoitred without delay. This patrol will not cross a line drawn due W. from the N. Corner of MAX WOOD. Their special mission is to deal with any hostile party who may be seen retiring E. after having been driven off by patrol (A). Strict attention must be paid to local protection. The Patrol will withdraw
BEFORE DAWN.

3-8-17.

Spencer Acklom
Lt Colonel
22° N.F.

PATROL ORDERS

for the night

5th/6th August.

("A"). 1 complete platoon under 2nd Lt PEACOCK with an additional Lewis Gun and team attached will move out from DRAGOON POST as soon as possible after dusk, reconnoitre through SOMERVILLE WOOD from West to East and relieve the platoon now in position there. 2nd Lt PEACOCK will send small reconnoitring patrols as follows:-
    1. To examine the crater at G.32.d.20.90 and then take up a position of observation about G.32.d.40.70.
    2. To examine MAX WOOD.
If both of the above parties report no enemy, 2nd Lt PEACOCK will move forward with his main patrol dropping one Lewis Gun and team about G.32.d.80.30 to cover his rear, and will take up a position about G.33.c.00.60 taking the usual precautions for local protection. Any hostile party seen will be engaged and driven back to their own lines, their point of entry being noted The patrol will return to SOMERVILLE WOOD before dawn and will remain there, the additional Lewis Gun being returned to Battn Headquarters.

("B"). A patrol of 1 complete platoon of "B" Company under 2nd Lt BROWN. ~~CURTIS~~ with an additional Lewis Gun will move out from CRESSY TRENCH as soon as possible after dusk and advance along the SOUTH side of the road to FISHER CRATER dropping one Lewis Gun and team about M.2.d.10.50 to cover their rear. The remainder of the patrol will take up a position about M.2.d.30.50 and will send scouts to examine FISHER CRATER and the banks, dugouts and disused trenches in M.2.d. Any hostile party seen will be engaged and if circumstances permit an effort will be made to head them NORTHWARDS up the valley in M.2.b. towards 2nd Lt PEACOCK'S patrol. "B" patrol will return to CRESSY TRENCH before dawn.

Spencer Acklom
Lt Colonel.

PATROL ORDERS

for the night
6th/7th August.

"A". A patrol of 1 complete platoon under 2nd Lt STOBBS with additional Lewis Gun attached will move out from DRAGOON POST as early as possible after dusk and reconnoitre through SOMERVILLE WOOD relieving the standing patrol already there. Small patrols will then be sent out to reconnoitre the crater at G.32.d.25.90 and MAX WOOD respectively and to remain out in observation near these points. If they report no enemy, the main patrol will move to a position from which it can observe the dugout and camouflaged trench reported about G.32.d.7.0. Any hostile party seen will at once be attacked and driven back to their own lines, their point of entry being particularly noted. The patrol will return to our lines before dawn, leaving one section and one Lewis Gun section in SOMERVILLE WOOD.

"B". A complete platoon under 2nd Lt BROWN will move out from CRESSY TRENCH as soon as possible after dusk and will take up a position about M.8.c.80.25. The platoon will attack any hostile party seen and drive them back to their own lines. In the event of a hostile enterprise being attempted against our picquet line between the CHIGNON RIVER and SALT TRENCH, 2nd Lt BROWN will co-operate with the garrison by attacking the enemy with fire. Should the enemy penetrate our line 2nd Lt BROWN's platoon will counter-attack him. If it should be necessary for the platoon to come into action within view of our picquet line 2nd Lt BROWN will arrange to fire ONE WHITE VERY LIGHT as a distinguishing signal.

[signature] Lt.Col.
O.C. 22nd N.F.

Patrol Orders tonight are modified as follows as far as they concern the patrols of 2nd Lts GRANT and STOBBS.

Our Artillery will fire tonight as follows:-

(a). 12-30 a.m. to 12-40 a.m. 13 pdrs. 100 rounds on ELEVEN TREES.

(b). 10.0 p.m. 10-20 p.m. 10-45 p.m. 18 pdrs. 5 rounds at each time stated on track through enemys wire at G.33.b.05.66.

(c). 12-35 a.m. 12-50 a.m. 1-15 a.m. 18 pdrs. 5 rounds at each time stated on track through enemys wire at G.33.d.00.57.

As soon as the firing mentioned in (a) is completed at 12-40 a.m. 2nd Lt GRANT will send forward a reconnoitring patrol of one N.C.O. and six men to examine ELEVEN TREES and bring in wounded or identifications if available.   In order to be able to support this party, he will move his platoon to about G.33.c.50.55 before 12-40 a.m.

The point at which 2nd Lt STOBBS will take up his position tonight will be about G.32.d.70.42 and not as previously detailed. He will thus be in a better position to cover 2nd Lt GRANT'S rear if required.

Spencer Acklom
Lt Colonel

PATROL ORDERS ⑥

for the night

8th/9th August.

"A". A patrol of 1 complete platoon under 2nd Lt GRANT with an additional Lewis Gun attached and a complete platoon under 2nd Lt STOBBS will rendezvous at LONE TREE POST at 8-30 p.m. and will commence moving to SOMERVILLE WOOD at the earliest possible moment after dusk. The patrol will move to DOG'S LEG WOOD to relieve the patrol already there, detaching 2nd Lt STOBBS' platoon to reconnoitre the crater at G.32.d.20.90 and take up a position about the cross roads at G.32.b.50.10.
The remainder of the patrol having carried out the relief will move to about G.33.c.12.12, their scouts reconnoitring in advance the dugouts at G.32.d.70.00 and MAX WOOD, and will lie up for the enemy, taking the usual precautions for local protection. 2nd Lt GRANT will post his second Lewis Gun about
G33 c 00.35 → ~~G.33.c.35.00~~ to guard his LEFT and REAR. 2nd Lt STOBBS and 2nd Lt GRANT will attack any hostile parties seen and will drive them to their own lines, their point of entry being noted.
2nd Lt STOBBS will withdraw his platoon to our lines before dawn. 2nd Lt GRANT will remain out during daylight on the 9th instant, either in the DUGOUTS at G.32.d.70.00 or in MAX WOOD. At dusk on the 9th inst he will move to DOG LEG WOOD, taking the usual precautions and throwing out standing patrols N., E., and S of his position. He will withdraw to our lines on relief.

"B". A patrol of 1 complete platoon under 2nd Lt MAUGHAN with an additional Lewis Gun attached will move out from CRESSY TRENCH as soon as possible after dusk by the road to FISHER CRATER taking the usual precautions for local protection, and will take up a position about M.2.d.52.52 leaving the second Lewis Gun about M.2.d.33.55 to cover their rear. 2nd Lt MAUGHAN will detach scouts to reconnoitre the wire round FISHER CRATER and dugouts and trenches in M.2.d. He will also detail a special patrol to reconnoitre the listening post at M.3.c.50.46 and report if it is occupied or wired.
Any hostile party seen will be attacked by the platoon and driven to their own lines, their point of entry being noted.
The patrol will withdraw to CRESSY TRENCH before dawn.

PATROL ORDERS.

for the night

9th/10th August.

(A).   A patrol of one complete platoon under 2nd.Lt. PEACOCK with
        an additional Lewis Gun attached, and a complete platoon under
        2nd.Lt. STOBBS will rendezvous at LONE TREE POST at 8.30 p.m.,
        and will commence moving to SOMERVILLE WOOD at the earliest
        possible moment after dusk.
        2nd.Lt. STOBBS' will post his platoon in SOMERVILLE WOOD,
        making thorough arrangements for observation N.- E. and S.
        2nd.Lt. PEACOCK after relieving 2nd.Lt. GRANT, will move his
        Platoon with due precautions to about G.33.c.00.40, placing his
        second Lewis Gun about G.32.d.90.40 to cover his FLANKS.

        2nd.Lt. PEACOCK will attack any hostile party sighted and
        will drive them to their own lines.   2nd.Lt. STOBBS will also
        engage any hostile party approaching him, but will make it his
        first duty to deny SOMERVILLE WOOD to the enemy and to protect
        2nd.Lt. PEACOCK'S rear.   The patrol will return to our lines
        before dawn, with the exception of 2 sections with a Lewis
        Gun from 2ndLt. PEACOCK'S platoon, who will remain in the
        SOMERVILLE WOOD AREA during daylight to-morrow in charge of
        a N.C.O.

(B).   2nd.Lt. MAUGHAN will carry out the same reconnaissance as
        last night with his platoon and an additional Lewis Gun.   He
        will in addition endeavour to enter and reconnoitre
        ST. HELEN'S TRENCH with a reconnoitring patrol, covered by
        a Lewis Gun which should be brought up close to the enemy
        wire at the point of entry to protect the line of withdrawal.
        If a sentry post is located near the point of entry, an effort
        may be made to capture it if this can be done without incurring
        undue risk.   The patrol will return to our lines before
        dawn.

Lt. Col.
Comdg 22nd N.F.

PATROL ORDERS
for the
night
20th/21st August.
****

"C" Company PATROL:-

A fighting patrol consisting of one complete platoon with Lewis Gun, under 2nd.Lt. PINGROME will move out from BENJAMIN POST at 1.30 a.m. with the object of attacking any hostile party met at CURNET COPSE or neighbourhood, where it is known hostile parties frequent.

From BENJAMIN POST, patrol will move along Valley in S.E. Direction, the right protecting scouts watching carefully the SUNKEN ROAD at F.24.c.7.5. and in the direction of CURNET High trench. On reaching F.24.c.95.65 patrol will, after taking usual precautions for local protection, send forward one group of scouts to the N. corner of CURNET COPSE at A.19.d.40.80, and another group to the S.W. edge of Copse at A.19.d.05.60.

Any enemy parties in the vicinity will be promptly fired on with Lewis Gun and rifle, and the ground reconnoitred where enemy were seen in order that identification may be secured.

"D" Company PATROL:-

From 1.30 a.m. to 4 a.m. a Fighting patrol consisting of 20 Other Ranks and Lewis Gun, provided with wire cutters will be sent out from RIFLEMAN POST to RIFLE PIT TRENCH. F.29.b.90.15, F.30.c.30.50. The object is to attack any hostile patrols that may be met, examine enemy wire, and cut as much loose hostile wire as possible.

[signature]
Capt.
Commdg. 3rd BATTALION TYNESIDE SCOTTISH,
(22nd (S) Bn. NORTHD. FUS:)

20-8-17.

Reference
NAUROY.
1/20,000.

PATROL ORDERS.
for the night
21st /22nd
August.

(9)

"B" COMPANY PATROL:-

From 9.30 p.m. to 1 a.m., a fighting patrol under 2nd.Lt.
provided with wire-cutters and Lewis Gun, will be sent out from
RIFLEMAN POST to RIFLE PIT TRENCH.
 The Object will be to attack any hostile patrol that may be met,
examine the enemy wire, and to cut gaps in wire between F.30.c.10.90
and F.30.c.40.60.
 Care will be taken not to pull out any angle irons or pickets,
but simply loosen them.

"C" COMPANY PATROL:-

 A Fighting patrol consisting of one complete platoon with Lewis
Gun, under 2nd.Lt.   , will move out from BENJAMIN POST
at 9.30 P.M. with the object of attacking any hostile patrol
met, and also reporting on the condition of the wire in front of
MALAKOFF SUPPORT TRENCH, from SOUTH Corner of QUENNET COPSE to
road at A.19.d.0.5.10.
 The Patrol from BENJAMIN POST will move in a S.E. direction to
fork roads at F.30.a.40.90, then follow the road which cuts
QUENNET HIGH TRENCH at F.30.a.65.95, taking the usual precautions for
flank protection before crossing the trench at this point. The
Lewis Gun should take up a position at F.30.a.65.95 to cover party
who go forward to enemy wire.

NOTE:-
 In future Map 1/20,000 NAUROY Sheet will be used for all references
for present normal operations and patrol reports.

                                            Capt.
                      Commndg. 3rd BATTALION TYNESIDE SCOTTISH.
                                    (22nd (S) Bn. NORTH'D FUS.)

21-8-17.

Ref. HAGNEY
Special
Sheet.
1/20,000.

PATROL ORDERS No 3
for night 24th/25th August
by
Major G. Charlton
Comdg. 22nd Bn Northumberland Fusiliers.

"C" COMPANY.

A Fighting patrol consisting of one complete platoon provided with wire cutters and Lewis Gun under 2nd Lt EDGELEY will move out from HUSSAR POST at 9.30 p.m.

OBJECT.

To attack any hostile party met in NO MANS LAND, to examine RIFLE PIT TRENCH and wire immediately West of it, from its junction with RIFLEMAN POST to about F.30.c.4.0 and to cut further gaps in hostile wire South of SUNKEN ROAD in F.30.c.

Patrol will not proceed further South than F.30.c.4.0.

O.C. LEFT GROUP DIV. ARTILLERY is arranging to fire frequent bursts on to RIFLE PIT TRENCH and wire immediately West of it on the front F.30c.8.8 to F.30.c.4.0 from 9.30 p.m. to 10.30 p.m. tonight 24th/25th.

Patrol will move out from HASSAR POST following the line of the Sunken Road running S.E. in F.29.d. as far as the cross roads at F.29.d.85.80., then following the line of Sunken Road running N.E. to F.30.c.05.30 where patrol will lie up until the Artillery lifts from RIFLE PIT TRENCH when patrol will promptly move forward, make necessary examination of wire and cut gaps in hostile wire West of RIFLE PIT TRENCH South of Sunken Road in F.30.c.

On return patrol will examine wire in front of RIFLE PIT TRENCH from F.30.c.4.5 to RIFLEMAN POST.

It is most imperative that a clear report should be given tonight on the condition of this wire. Any hostile patrols met will be immediately attacked and fired on by rifle and Lewis Gun, and identification secured if possible.

Patrol must be within our lines by midnight 24th/25th.

24.8.17.
Comdg.
Major.

3rd BATTALION TYNESIDE SCOTTISH
(22nd (S) Bn. NORTHD. FUS)

Copies to
No. 1. "A" Coy.
  2. "B" "
  3. "C" "
  4. 102nd Brigade.
  5. 23rd N.F.
  6. Liaison Officer, R.F.A.
  7. War Diary.
  8. Retained.

Army Form C. 2118.

WAR DIARY
or
INTELLIGENCE SUMMARY
(Erase heading not required.)

Volume 21. 22/9/16
Sheet 55. Notts & Derby

Vol 21

Place	Date	Hour	Summary of Events and Information	Remarks and references to Appendices
HARDECOURT	Sept 1		Battalion still in supp. Salvador, 102nd & 8th Bn front. Continued on the consolidation of the newly captured positions. Trench (Craisford line) had been badly damaged in our artillery preparation. A good deal of work was carried out on this trench by our forward companies. Early morning attack to be made in the open on the left of the position, following the line of a ring shelter trench - AIP LANE - to ONION trench. This trench was therefore my induce our supporters between C.T. and almost due East & West from the SUNKEN ROAD at L.6.C.55.10 forms POND TRENCH at G.1.N.40.15. Strong parties were also constructed in POND TRENCH to protect the garrison from enfilade M. Gun and artillery fire from the direction of the junction of RAILWAY FARM TRENCHES also beyond QUARRY WOOD which the enemy still held. Our trenches looked on the flanks of our positions	Ref map GUILLEMONT FARM PARIS SP 57 C SE 57 & SW 62 C NE 62 C NW. Casualties Wounded 7 OR

Place	Date	Hour	Summary of Events and Information	Remarks and references to Appendices
AARICOURT	Sept 2	CONT'D	Our pickets still further out and our right flank in RAILWAY TRIANGLE secured by the supping of a new trench on a S.W. direction connecting RAILWAY TRENCH with (NEW) No 6 POST at L.12.C.85.80	
do			Battalion relieved in Left Sub-sector 102nd BDE front by 11th SUFFOLKS 101st Brigade. The Battalion on relief marched to BERNES where accommodation was found in huts.	"Joined 3.9.17. 2Lt A.T.B. BEGG " J.E.M. GRANT " E. RYLE " F.G. OLIVER " D.A. ROGERS " J. POTTS
BERNES	3		Battalion in huts	
"	4		Training being carried out. Rifles ranged MERILLY made by Commander with Returns in afternoon for Battalion Officers. Pool shooting in morning on RIFLE RANGE.	
"	5		Orders were received that D ..... will be employed on digging + carrying work in forthcoming operations by 102 Bde in connection with the further extension of our gains SOUTH of COLOGNE RIDGE.	
"	6		Battalion still in same area lent to D.. Company who now moved	

WAR DIARY or INTELLIGENCE SUMMARY

Army Form C. 2118.

Sheet 57.

Place	Date	Hour	Summary of Events and Information	Remarks and references to Appendices
BERNES	Contd		up the Intermediate Line behind VILLERET. The Company was working with 108 Bde instructions in the construction of Sap, Grenade + R.E. dumps.	
"	7.		Battalion less "D" Company still in billets at BERNES. "D" Company (Mason + Company) training carried out until	
VILLARET	8		On the night of 7th & 8th Sept. 1914 the Battalion less "D" Company, who are already in the VILLARET area engaged and finding carrying parties under 102 Brigade instructions moved up to a position 800 yards South of VILLARET proceeding via JEANCOURT. At 12.30am the 21st N.F. (3rd T.S.) and 23rd N.F. (4th T.S.) attacked the enemy positions in FARM TRENCH, east of VILLARET. The object of the attack was (1) to gain and consolidate a line which will give extension to the Quarry Wood and the Quarry South of it (2) to deny the the enemy observation east into QUARRY RAVINE, into the Valley North of VILLARET also on attack and provide a C.T. and for flank defence from FARM TRENCH.	

WAR DIARY or INTELLIGENCE SUMMARY

Army Form C. 2118.

Place	Date	Hour	Summary of Events and Information	Remarks and references to Appendices
VILLARET (CONT'D)	8		About G.B.I. 85.80 & MARTIN POST and to hung under orders to 22nd N.F. on the with two Companies 22nd N.F. ("A"C) and the platoons of two Platoons 12th YORKS. PIONEERS, altogether a Fighting Strength of 150 men, were allotted for this both. The attack was supported by 5th Divisional artillery augmented for the Operation and ordered under fire of 24 VICKERS Guns. The left attacking Battalion 23rd N.F. (4 K.T.S.) seized the whole of this Objective. In the right Bn which provided the right Company of the right Battalion ie 21st N.F. (2nd T.S.) rather lost direction. Consequently the Battalion did not secure the whole of FARM TRENCH on its frontage allotted to them. Owing to very heavy hostile barrage suffering was experienced in communication and some time elapsed before it was known where the right flank of 21st N.F. actually was. Definite information was eventually received at 3.5 a.m. that was found that the front line FARM TRENCH (G.B.I. 85.80) from which were — C.T.R.K.	Casualties: 2/Lt. J. LAING "E RYLE Both wounded OR. Killed 2 OR. Wounded 15
	9	12.15 am		

(A7092) Wt. W12539/M1293. 75/000. 1/17. D.D. & L. Ltd. Forms/C.2118/14.

WAR DIARY
or
INTELLIGENCE SUMMARY.
(Erase heading not required.) Sheet 59

Army Form C. 2118.

Place	Date	Hour	Summary of Events and Information	Remarks and references to Appendices
VILLARET (CONT?)	9th		dug by 22nd N.F. and to form the lateral trench 6.20 still in enemy hands. At 8.30am runner orders was issued by C.O. 22nd N.F. (Major Challen) that digging should be commenced immediately from MARTIN POST towards G.7.d.95.25 where it was known right flank of 21st N.F. was established. About 200 yards of trench 2 feet deep was dug from MARTIN POST towards FARM TRENCH. At 5.0am both enemy and our own to day light. The work could no longer be continued owing to heavy shelling throughout the whole of this time some most severe enemy shelling. No M.G.'s and our mounts of a heavy barrage falling in the spinneys no shelling MARTIN POST. "B" Coy during the spinneys were also in reserve at BATT. H.Q. L.23.f.5.6. coming under use of H.Q. 21st N.F. (H.Q. Floyd). They were not made use of	
		6.0am	Orders were received from G.O.C. 109 Brigade to move to "A" & "B" battalions, 22nd N.F. to 2 Platoons Marigone Park also "B" Coy 22nd N.F. YORKSHIRE PIONEERS. Each INTERMEDIATE LINE + nr FERVAQUE FARM. We were not form a BRIGADE RESERVE.	

WAR DIARY
INTELLIGENCE SUMMARY

Army Form C. 2118.

Sheet 60

Place	Date	Hour	Summary of Events and Information	Remarks and references to Appendices
VILLARET (CONTD)	9		"D" Company 22nd N.F. still to remain in their present position at L.7.A.3.4 furnishing carrying parties under orders 102nd Inf Bde.	
do	9	10.0 p.m.	B + C Companies 22nd N.F. digging new C.T. from No. 6 (NEW) POST, VILLARET connecting up RAILWAY TRENCH at G.7.d.65.95. "A" Company in reserve at FERVAQUE TRENCH. D Company still engaged as above.	
do	10	2.30 p.m.	C.O. 22nd N.F. attended conference together with C.O. 21st N.F. summoned by Brigade Commander, 102 Inf Bde. As a result of this conference it was decided that the 22nd N.F. in conjunction with 21st N.F. should attack the enemy's position in FARM TRENCH on the front G.13.A.95.75 (M.Gun emplacement inclusive) to Block in trench at G.7.d.95.35. While the right flank of 21st N.F. then rested. The operation was to consist of a man attack on the frontage G.13.A.95.75-to G.13.A.95.90 (enemy C.T. inclusive) by B + C Companies 22nd N.F. under Capt MARK D.S.O., M.C. Whilst by Major Geo. CHARLTON the 21st N.F. were to co-operate	See G.O. 2nd N.F. should 141 attacks Casualties O.R. Wounded 3

Army Form C. 2118.

WAR DIARY
or
INTELLIGENCE SUMMARY.
(Erase heading not required.)

Sheet 61

Place	Date	Hour	Summary of Events and Information	Remarks and references to Appendices
MILLERET (OUD)	15/11	11 p.m.	From the NORTH by a tawny attack down FARM TRENCH and the 22nd N.F. would no silence for the SOUTH were taking up the flanks of the Battalion. A forming up place for the attack was chosen 100 yards and EAST of MARTIN POST by O.C. Battalion. The right of "C" Company was ordered to direct and advance on a compass bearing of 90° (true). Tapes at the forming up point were carefully laid out before hand. Lieut. G.R. Brown was placed in charge of the tape party. D Coy	
		3.0 a.m.	ZERO was fixed at 3.0 am and at this hour the assaulting troops advanced to the attack. Everywhere we secured our objectives and a total of 25 prisoners was captured including a Company Sergt Major of the 167 I.R. Two M. Guns also fell into our hands also a large quantity of rifles, grenades, etc.	

WAR DIARY
or
INTELLIGENCE SUMMARY.

Army Form C. 2118.

Sheet 62

Place	Date	Hour	Summary of Events and Information	Remarks and references to Appendices
VILLARET (CONT'D)	11		Our casualties in the forming up and actual attack are NIL, the enemy being taken completely by surprise. The enemy suffered heavily, a large number were accounted for in the trench itself and a good many Boche who fled to the rear were killed by our barrage. A good number of enemy prisoners and to our two were killed in the neighbourhood of T.LL MRET by hostile barrage.	Casualties 2/Lt. W.A. COWDEN Wounded (at duty) O.R. Killed 3 O.R. Wounded 13.
		9.30a.	Enemy counter attacked from neighbourhood of QUARRY WOOD and from the continuation of FARM TRENCH on our right flank. The enemy came on in close formation and heavy masses and were met by rifle Lewis gun fire. These counter attacks were completely smashed, and were not retained again during the day. At 12.30p.m. the 22nd N.F. hooked onto the portion of FARM TRENCH held by 21st N.F. on the left flank, thus connecting up with 23rd N.F. at the Junction of RAILWAY FARM trenches. The 22nd N.F. then	

WAR DIARY
or
INTELLIGENCE SUMMARY.

Army Form C. 2118.

Sheet 63

Place	Date	Hour	Summary of Events and Information	Remarks and references to Appendices
VILLRET (cont'd)	11	—	Holding right Battalion of the CENTRE SECTOR, 34th Division front.	
		3.30p	Warning orders received from 102nd B'de. Battalion will be relieved by 11th SUFFOLKS of 101 Inf. Bde.	
	12	2.30a.m	Battalion relieved by 11th SUFFOLKS. On relief Battalion marched to billets at ROISEL.	

			The following Officers N.C.O's men and stretcher bearers work among the dead of the operations, displaying great endurance and gallantry, the whole carried during an example of fine soldierly qualities.
			
			Capt. MARK ASO. M.C.
			Sec Lieut. R.B. STEPHENSON } 'C' Company
			  do. B. PEACOCK 'A' do.
			  do. G.A. BROWN D do.
			  do. E. MOYES D do.
			22/7442 Sgt. HERBERT STUTTARD
			22/194 " (A/Coy.CSM.) THOMAS TODD
			20/54 Pte. George CURRY
			39730 Lance Cpl. E.T. STYAN	

WAR DIARY
INTELLIGENCE SUMMARY.

Army Form C. 2118.

Sheet 64

Place	Date	Hour	Summary of Events and Information	Remarks and references to Appendices
VILLERET (CONTD)	12		Congratulatory messages received from III Corps, 34th Division & 102nd Bde Commanders in connection with the execution of the very successful operation. The Battalion on this occasion was most ably supported by the LEFT GROUP, 34th Divisional artillery (Lt Col NIMBURTON D.S.O.), and Overhead indirect M.Gun fire by 102nd M. Gun Corps.	
ROISEL.	13		Battalion in billets	
"	14		102nd Inf Bde inspected, but decorations presented to Officers, NCO's &men by Lt. General SIR W.P. POULTENEY, K.C.B, K.C.M.G, D.S.O. commanding III CORPS.	
"	15		Battalion still in billets. Liaison Company having carried out	Draft 14 OR. Joined 15.7.17
"	16		do	

Army Form C. 2118.

WAR DIARY
or
INTELLIGENCE SUMMARY.
(Erase heading not required.)

Sheet 65

Instructions regarding War Diaries and Intelligence Summaries are contained in F. S. Regs. Part II and the Staff Manual respectively. Title pages will be prepared in manuscript.

Place	Date	Hour	Summary of Events and Information	Remarks and references to Appendices
ROISEL	17	—	Battalion move forward to the line and relieve the 24/27 N.F. in the night. Sub sector of the left sector 34th Divisional front. Dispositions D & A forward companies B Coy support C Coy Battalion reserve. Battalion Headquarters at L.11.a.35.85.	Drafts joined 54 OR 9 OR
HARGICOURT	18 19 20 21 22	—	Battalion still in the sector. During our tour a new trench dug from G.1.d.60.85 to G.1.d.70.45 connecting FISH LANE with BAIT TRENCH. The wire on the whole of our front strengthened and pushed out further from our parapet. Standing blocks and loop hole houses constructed in BAIT TRENCH. Battalion snipers & S.A.A store reorganised. Large quantities of ammunition along collected and returned to salvage dump. FISH LANE & BAIT TRENCH were gassed. Our patrols were out in NO MAN'S LAND nightly. On one occasion one of our enemy patrol encountered and this latter immediately retired towards their own line or when fired on by	Casualties O.R. Wounded 4 7745 P. DEEGAN Joined 19.9.17

Army Form C. 2118.

WAR DIARY
or
INTELLIGENCE SUMMARY.
(Erase heading not required.)

Sheet 66

Place	Date	Hour	Summary of Events and Information	Remarks and references to Appendices
ARGICOURT (CAVES)	22		Whole Bn. out. All preparing did good work in the construction and strengthening on position.	
do.	22		Battalion relieved in left sector of 34th Bgde Divisional front on night of 22/23 Sept 1917 by 21st M.F. (2nd. Tyneside Scotch) on relief Battalion accommodated in shelters near ARGICOURT QUARRY (L.10.a.55.) and furnishing carrying and supping parties nightly.	Draft 20 OR joined 23/9/17
do.	23		Battalion furnished carrying & digging parties each night.	
do.	24			
do.	25			
HANCOURT	26		Battalion relieved in Brigade Reserve, left sector of 34th Divisional front by 2nd Lincolns. On relief Battalion proceeded by march route to billets in HANCOURT.	Draft 9 OR joined 26/9/17
DOINGT	27		Battalion moved from Hancourt to billets in DOINGT by busses.	

Army Form C. 2118.

WAR DIARY
or
INTELLIGENCE SUMMARY.
(Erase heading not required.)

Sheet 67.

Place	Date	Hour	Summary of Events and Information	Remarks and references to Appendices
DOINGT.	28.		The Corps Commander inspected a parade consisting of 1 Company from each Battalion, the following from this Battalion, received the Military Medal :— 200818 Pte. J. Thistle 266104 " H. Robson 21/911 " (a/cpl) E. J. Sanderson 21/927 L/Spl. St. Davison 204559 Pte. W. Lawson 242896 Sergt. J. Ratcliffe 22/94 Sergt (a/C.S.M.) T. Todd. 22273 Pte (a/Cpl. W. McGuinness 22/896 Pte. J. Morley.	Draft 9/191 O.R. joined 28.7.17
BAILLEULVAL.	29.		Battalion vacated billets in DOINGT and marched to PERONNE where it entrained & proceeded by rail to BOISLEUX, from there by route march to billets in BAILLEULVAL.	
do	30		Battalion in rest area for purpose of training	

Spencer Acklom Lt Col
Cy 3rd BATTALION TYNESIDE SCOTTISH
(22nd (S) Bn. NORTHD. FUS.)

Secret.

Ref. Map
Special C.T.S.
Map No 101
1/10,000 d/4.9.17
NAUROY SHEET.
1/20,000.

Operation Orders No 141
by
Major Geo Charlton
commdg. 22nd Bn Northld Fus.

Intention 1. The 22nd. N.F. in conjunction with 21st N.F will capture and consolidate the enemy's positions in FARM trench on the front G.13.b.95.75 (M.G. Emplacement inclusive) to BLOCK at G.7.d.95.35.

Attack 2. The operations will consist of —

(a) A main attack on the frontage G.13.b.95.75 to G.13.b.95.90 (enemy C.T. inclusive) by "B" and "C" Coys 22nd. N.F under Capt Mark, D.S.O, M.C. "A" Coy 22nd. N.F less special wiring party, will be in reserve at L.23.b.5.5.

(b) After capture of this objective a flank bombing attack from the NORTH at G.7.d.95.35 to G.13.b.95.90 by 21st N.F. G.7.d.05.95 ~

(c) Should patrols of ~~a gap still exist between~~ "B" Coy. 22nd N.F and 21st N.F be unable to establish touch a bombing attack will be made by "B" Coy, 22nd N.F at ZERO plus 45", and 21st N.F will simultaneously do likewise to link up. Two White Very Lights fired in quick succession will be the signal used by these bombing parties as they close inwards.

Consolidation 3. The consolidation of the captured trench will be commenced immediately and will be covered on frontage of 22nd N.F by parties as previously detailed provided with Lewis Guns pushed out 80 yards to the East of FARM trench. The right groups provided by "C" Coy will face S.E and watch the right flank. Double blocks will also be established in FARM trench by "C" Coy, 22nd N.F at about G.13.b.98.68. also by "B" Coy in C.T. at about G.14.a.05.90.
The right flank of the captured position will be protected by a short trench ~~sighted~~ sited for flank defence from FARM trench at G.13.b.95.73.

Artillery 4. The attack will be supported by Field Guns, medium & heavy Hows.
Field gun barrage as follows :-

    ZERO until ZERO plus 2 — QUARRY TRENCH
    ZERO plus 2 until ZERO plus 4 —
                INTERMEDIATE NEW TRENCH.
    ZERO plus 4 until ZERO plus 6 —
                FARM TRENCH.

At ZERO plus 6 the Field Gun barrage lifts from FARM trench and forms a protective barrage 150 yards East of FARM trench. Howitzers will cover FARM trench from - G.14.a.05.55 Southwards

Trench Mortars 5. One Stokes Mortar will be at disposal of Capt. Mark, after position has been captured, to be used as detailed.

Machine Guns.	6.	The attack will be supported by overhead indirect M. Gun fire.
Aeroplane Co-operation	7.	Flares will be carried and lighted when called for by aeroplanes.
ZERO.	8.	Zero hour will be notified later.
Direction	9.	The right of "C" Coy will direct & march on magnetic bearing of 102° taken from centre of Cross Roads at MARTIN POST.
Communication	10.	A receiving lamp station will be established at L.23.b.75.90.
Forming up	11.	Companies will form up in No Mans Land with the right of "C" Coy on C.13.b.23.72 the left of "B" Coy being 75 yards true North of this point.
Dress.	12.	As detailed, less entrenching tool and shaft. Covers for Steel helmets will be worn by all ranks.
Prisoners.	13.	A Collecting Post is being established at L.23.b.5.5. Escorts not to exceed 10% of the prisoners.
Medical	14.	Regimental Aid Post will be established at Quarry L.23.b.5.5.
	15.	Acknowledge.

(Signed) J. Fulton.
Capt
A/Adjutant

10 Sept. 1917.
Issued at 10 pm.
Distribution
No 1   Retained
   2   A Coys
   3   B "
   4   C "
   5   D "
   6   21st N.F.
   7   102nd Bde
   8   War Diary

WAR DIARY
or
INTELLIGENCE SUMMARY.
(Erase heading not required.)

Army Form C. 2118.

Place	Date	Hour	Summary of Events and Information	Remarks and references to Appendices
BAILLEULVAL	Oct 1-6		Battalion in rest area for purpose of training. Each morning were devoted to musketry, rifle grenade instruction, Lewis gun instruction and extended order drill. Special training of the men of the new draft was carried out in the afternoons. Sports were organised and inter-platoon matches were played daily. There was an instructional class for N.C.O's every morning in lieu of the running parades witt often were attended.	Joined 2.10.17 2/Lt Mr Dunn 2/Lt A.E. Kell Draft 10 OR
	7-8		The battalion vacated billets in BAILLEULVAL and marched to SAULTY STATION where it entrained and proceeded by rail to PESELHOEK, from thence by march route to POLHILL CAMP	
POLHILL CAMP	9 10 11 12		Battalion remained in camp and training. The special features of its training there were (i) leapfrog attack (ii) Counter-attack in the open and (iii) method of capturing a "pill box".	
	13		Battalion vacated POLHILL CAMP and marched to PROVEN STATION, entrained to ELVERDINGHE STATION whence it proceeded by route march to BRIDGE CAMP	
ELVERDINGHE	14		The Battalion vacated BRIDGE CAMP and marched to LEIPZIG CAMP and stayed there one night. — As companies were proceeding in to LEIPZIG Camp hostile Aeroplanes flew over and dropped bombs, causing no 5 casualties. — Heavy casualties were inflicted at the same time upon other troops in the vicinity. —	

WAR DIARY or INTELLIGENCE SUMMARY

Army Form C. 2118. Sheet 69.

Place	Date	Hour	Summary of Events and Information	Remarks and references to Appendices
LANGEMARCK	15th		The Battalion drew S.A.A. Iron rations, Sandbags, etc. to complete for active operations & moved forward to bivouacs near STRAY FARM, less 'D' Coy which occupied EAGLE TRENCH. — Orders received for move into the line tomorrow to relieve 24/27th N.F. —	
	16th	6 am	O.C. and Company Commanders reconnoitered forward area. —	
		5.30pm	Battalion moved off to 'B' Track, platoon marching at 200 yds distance led by guides of 24/27th N.F. — Enemy shelling edge of the track. — Battalion took over line from V14.a.02.49. – 26.0.97. W of HELLES HOUSE — to the WATERVLIETBEEK about 250 yds W of RUBENS FARM in V8.c. — Disposition from RIGHT to LEFT A, C, B Coys with D Coy in support behind A Coy. — Battn H.Qrs at FERDAN HOUSE in V19.a. — The 24/27 N.F. had only occupied the line for 24 hours and much difficulty and delay was experienced in relieving owing to their guides proving unable to find the routes to their companies. — This resulted in unnecessary casualties and we were unable to relieve 2 platoons of the 24/27th N.F. who were then compelled to remain in the line until the evening of the 17th. — Our H.Q. Platoon was unable to & judge in the track area from after leaving STRAY FARM and did not come up till 24 hours later. —	
POELCAPPELLE	17th		Our positions were very heavily shelled at various times both by day & night. — LANDING FARM, the H.Q. of 'C' Coy was set on fire by an incendiary shell & destroyed. —	
	18th	At 5 am today 'A' Coy reported that the MIDDLESEX Regt. on our RIGHT had fallen back before dawn, thus leaving our flank exposed. — Subsequently enquiries	

WAR DIARY or INTELLIGENCE SUMMARY

Army Form C. 2118.

Sheet 70.

Place	Date	Hour	Summary of Events and Information	Remarks and references to Appendices
			that they had received orders to withdraw 200 yds before daylight in order to permit of our artillery bombarding the enemy, strong points on the Western fringe of POELCAPPELLE. — Owing to our field Batteries firing 200 yds short the MIDDLESEX were compelled to continue their withdrawal as far as the Western edge of the POELCAPPELLE — S'CHEMINS ROAD. — We reported the situation to the 102 Bde who had up 2 additional VICKERS guns to cover our exposed flank. — The hostile shelling was still more violent today in reply to our bombardment. — The enemy front system of defence consist of organized shell holes and PILL BOXES and do appear to hold any light by day and in considerable strength by night. — A company of the 20th N.F. relieved our 'B' (LEFT) company tonight. — 'B' Coy then withdrew to EAGLE TRENCH, but suffered 15 casualties from GAS on route. — MIDDLESEX on our RIGHT are being relieved tonight. —	
	19th		The condition of the men is becoming more and more serious owing to exposure and the lack of Rations and water. — Brigade have sent a warning that the enemy is preparing an attack on a large scale and may use Tanks. — A readjustment of the Divisional Frontage is to take place tonight. — Our RIGHT Coy ('A') is to be relieved by the 8th NORTHANTS and we are to take over a fresh portion of line on our LEFT from the 20th N.F. —	
		10 p.m.	Relief carried out. — Our front is now approximately from LANDING FARM to BOWER HOUSE inclusive. — 'A' Company with guns on relief to STRAY FARM and 'D' Coy is moved back to the LEFT of C. —	

Army Form C. 2118.

WAR DIARY
or
INTELLIGENCE SUMMARY.
(Erase heading not required.)

Sheet 7.

Instructions regarding War Diaries and Intelligence Summaries are contained in F. S. Regs., Part II. and the Staff Manual respectively. Title pages will be prepared in manuscript.

Place	Date	Hour	Summary of Events and Information	Remarks and references to Appendices
LANGEMARCK	20th		Orders received for relief of our companies in the line by the 24th/27th N.F. tonight. — 2/Lt MOYES is taking guides to meet the incoming battalion at BON GITE. —	O.O. 164 B.M. 347
	21st		The relief last night was carried out with comparative ease, though its completion was not reported to Batt. H.Q. till 6 am. This morning owing to a runner losing his way in the dark. — The Battalion is now concentrated in Bivouacs W of STRAY FARM — Battalion H.Q. have been ordered back to the CANAL BANK. — The 101st and 103rd Brigades are carrying out an attack tomorrow. — 22 N.F. remains in reserve ready to move at 30 minutes notice. —	Total Casualties: Killed - OR. 17. D. of Wds. OR. 4 Wounded, OR. 75 Gassed, OR. 56 Missing, OR. 7 2/Lt J.H. Nicholson wounded 17.10.17 2/Lt. D.A. Rogers missing 20.10.17. 2/Lt. R.B. Heppenstall wounded 20.10.17 d. of wds. 23.10.17
	22nd	7pm	Orders received for battalion to move forward to WHITE TRENCH in U23c6. — This move was carried out about 7pm. and only about 180 O.R. were found fit to march. — The remainder continued to occupy the STRAY FARM area. —	
	23rd	9-	The Battalion is being withdrawn tonight to BOESINGHE Station in readiness for entrainment tomorrow. — A hot meal is being prepared for all ranks there. —	
	24th		The Batt. entrained this morning & proceeded by rail to PROVEN and thence by road to POLL HILL CAMP.	Draft 44 O.R. joined 25.10.17

WAR DIARY
or
INTELLIGENCE SUMMARY.
(Erase heading not required.)

Army Form C. 2118.

Sheet 72

Place	Date	Hour	Summary of Events and Information	Remarks and references to Appendices
POLL HILL CAMP	Oct 25, 26, 27, 28, 29		Battalion at rest. 32 men were from training in the Lewis Gun otherwise no other work was done. Battalion left POLL HILL CAMP marched to HOPOUTRE, when it entrained for BOISLEUX AUX MONT. On arrival the Battalion marched to the NORTHUMBERLAND LINES near MERCATEL.	21-10-17 2/Lt Pincock to Regime reposted Battn 2/Lt Fry 5 O.R.
NORTHUMBERLAND LINES	30		One officer from each company and Battalion Headquarters reconnoitred forward area.	
	31		Covering parties of Lewis Gunners, Observers, Dischargers sent forward.	
	Nov 1			

Spencer Cooban
Lt Col.

Cg 3rd BATTALION TYNESIDE SCOTTISH.
(22nd (S) Bn. NORTHD. FUS:)

Ref: My 51 R.S.W.

WAR DIARY
or
INTELLIGENCE SUMMARY.
(Erase heading not required.)

Army Form C. 2118.

22NF
Volume 23
Page 73

Place	Date	Hour	Summary of Events and Information	Remarks and references to Appendices
NORTHUMBER-LAND LINES	Nov. 1	9.30 a.m.	The Battalion moved off by platoons at an interval of 200' in order to relieve the 2nd Bn. Duke of Wellington's Regiment in the Right Sub-sector of the new 34th Divisional Front, the Battalion Front being from O.26.a.5765 to O.20.b.10.23. The disposition of the Battalion were 'D' Right Forward Coy. 'A' Left Forward Coy, 'B' Coy in Support, 'C' Coy in Reserve, with Battalion Hdqrs. in BUCK RESERVE.	CASUALTIES O.Rs. 6 Wounded (4 at duty)
GUEMAPPE YORK LINES M.22.B.9.3 (Ref. MAP Sheet 51b.S.W.)	Nov. 5		The Battalion was relieved by the 20th Northumberland Fusiliers (1st Tyneside Scottish) and on relief marched to York Lines and became Battalion in Brigade Reserve. Special training was given to Lewis gunners and rifle grenadiers.	
Batn. H.Q. BUCK RESERVE O.20.a.34	Nov. 9th		The Battalion left YORK LINES in the evening and marched to the Trenches relieving the 20th Northumberland Fusiliers (1st Tyneside Scottish) in the right Subsector of the left sector of 34th Divn. sail Regt. Our disposition were as follows:- Right Forward Company 'C', Left Forward Company 'A', Support 'B', Reserve 'D' Company. We again had a quiet tour, some useful information was found by patrols, British work was done improving the trenches particularly in area accupied by right forward company.	

A.S.634 Wt. W4973/M687 750,000 8/16 D.D.&L. Ltd. Forms/C.2118/13.

Army Form C. 2118.

WAR DIARY
or
INTELLIGENCE SUMMARY.
(Erase heading not required.)

Feb 17

Instructions regarding War Diaries and Intelligence Summaries are contained in F. S. Regs., Part II. and the Staff Manual respectively. Title pages will be prepared in manuscript.

Place	Date	Hour	Summary of Events and Information	Remarks and references to Appendices
Reserve R.151b S.W.	Nov 13		On morning of November 13th (after a 4 days 'tour in the line) the Battn. was relieved by the 20th Northumberland Fusiliers (1st Tyneside Scottish). One relief the Battn. moved into Bryant support. Disposition was as follows: 'A', 'B' and 'D' Companies were accommodated in shelters and dug-outs in N: 16.C.9. Battn. Headqrs. and C Company worked parties in the forward area. 'C' Coy. had 4 days rest and Light Training.	2/Lt KELL. R.E. transf. 9/NF
Batn. Hd.Qrs. Qu 9 d.5.4 Block Reserve	Nov 17		The Battn. moved forward into the line again relieving the 20th Northumberland Fusiliers (1st Tyneside Scottish) in the same area. Our disposition were as follows:- D Coy in Front Coy, B' Left Front Coy, A' Coy in Support - C' Coy in Reserve -	CASUALTIES 6 O.R. Killed 3 O.Rs. Wounded 2/Lt Watts Wounded 2/Lt Warwick wounded (at duty)
	18		There was a lot of enemy activity on both sides. Our Artillery activity has been somewhat above normal. I visit of the forthcoming operations by the 5th Army S.O. our position preparation have been completed to enable us to advance without delay in the event of the enemy retiring from this front.	
	19		No occurrence of special importance.	

Army Form C. 2118.

WAR DIARY
or
INTELLIGENCE SUMMARY.
(Erase heading not required.)

Sheet 75

Place	Date	Hour	Summary of Events and Information	Remarks and references to Appendices
	20		Considerable activity on our front this morning. - Gas projectors being used by us on a large scale. - The enemy put down a barrage in reply to this which caused a few casualties. -	
	21.		Our patrols have been very active by night along the whole front, and have reported the enemy to be holding his line as usual. -	
	22.		Situation unchanged - The enemy is still in his front system -	
YORK LINES M.22.b.9.3.	23.		The Battalion was relieved today by the 20th N.F. and moved back to YORK LINES becoming the Batt. in Brigade Reserve. -	
Batt. H.Q. O.10.a.3.4.	27		The Battalion relieved the 20th N.F. in the RIGHT (ARTOIS) Sub Sector. -	JOINED 27-11-17 2/Lt. G. KEENAN 2/Lt. R.L. NISBET.
	28.		We used GAS projectors on this front at 8.30 p.m. - At about midnight two of the enemy were found near our wire in front of "H" Post and were brought in by the garrison. -	JOINED 28-11-17 Capt. F.O. PADDELEY
	29.		Enemy artillery has been more active -	

Army Form C.

WAR DIARY
or
INTELLIGENCE SUMMARY.
(Erase heading not required)

Dec 76

Instructions regarding War Diaries and Intelligence Summaries are contained in F. S. Regs., Part II. and the Staff Manual respectively. Title pages will be prepared in manuscript.

Place	Date	Hour	Summary of Events and Information	Remarks and references to Appendices
	30.		An aeroplane bearing British markings flew over our lines at 2 pm to day and dropped two small bombs on the trenches occupied by our Support Company.	

James Knowles
Lt Colonel
Commg 22 NF.

WAR DIARY or INTELLIGENCE SUMMARY

22 NF
Volume 24
Sheet 77

Army Form C. 2118.

Place	Date	Hour	Summary of Events and Information	Remarks and references to Appendices
	Dec 1		The Battalion relieved the 20th N.F. in the RIGHT (ARTOIS) Subsector. The Battalion was in Brigade Support H.Q. and D Company at CARLISLE LINES (M16.b.9.5.) and A, B and C Companies at N.16.c. The three companies at N.16.c. were employed on working parties. D Company trained for a proposed raid – using trenches West of YORK LINES (M22.b.9.3.)	
	2nd			
	3rd			
	4th			
	3rd		"D" Company was inspected by Corps Commander. The Divisional Commander and Brigadier were present.	
	5th		The Battalion less "D" Company relieved the 20th N.F. in the RIGHT (ARTOIS) Subsector. The dispositions of the Companies were "C" Right Forward Company; "A" Left Forward Company; "B" Support Company. One Company of the Support Battalion (21st N.F.) became Reserve Company	
Bn. H.Q. O.20.a.3.4	6th 7th 8th 9th 10th		Patrols continue to actively reconnoitre the enemy wire and front line. The proposed raid being cancelled "D" Company relieves the Company of 21st N.F. becoming the Reserve Company Situation remained unchanged. Battalion relieved the 20th N.F. in the Right (ARTOIS) Sector and became Reserve Battalion at YORK LINES	
YORK LINES (M22.b.9.3)	10th		The day was spent cleaning equipment – baths and inning of men's clothes. The Commanding Officer conferred with Company Commanders and arranged a programme of training	

WAR DIARY
or
INTELLIGENCE SUMMARY.
(Erase heading not required.)

Army Form C. 2118.

Sheet 78.

Place	Date	Hour	Summary of Events and Information	Remarks and references to Appendices
YORK LINES	Dec 10th		About 4 p.m. the Adjutant was summoned to Brigade. He returned with information that attack by the Enemy was anticipated any morning and orders that the Battalion was to "stand to" each morning from 6.30 a.m. until orders to "stand down". Extra Bombs and S.A.A. were issued. Lewis guns and panniers were kept loaded on the limbers. Equipments were reassembled and every preparation made for a sudden hour.	
	11th		The Battalion stood to at 6 a.m. and as "Stand down" was not ordered till 11.30 a.m. owing to heavy mist, the training was not carried out. Wiring in the forward area was allotted to "D" Company as the Majority of "A" Company – for the night. A programme of training was drawn up for the two remaining companies for the following day.	
	12th		"A" and "D" Companies remained at MALIERES CAVES under Capt W Brown as O.C. Detachment. At about 6 a.m. "B" Company had orders to N16.c. on account of Enemy activity South of our sector. The Battalion stood to at 6 a.m. and "C" Company spent the morning after stand down – in training.	
	13th		Detachment remained at MALIERE CAVES to complete wiring and "B" Company at N.16.c. found a working party on 14/12/17	Casualties 1 O.R. Wounded

WAR DIARY
or
INTELLIGENCE SUMMARY.
(Erase heading not required.)

Army Form C. 2118.

Sheet 79.

Place	Date	Hour	Summary of Events and Information	Remarks and references to Appendices
HENIN CAMP (N.26.d.4.0.20)	14th		102nd Brigade relieved the 103rd Brigade in Reserve. The Battalion relieved the 9th Batts N.F. and moved to HENIN CAMP (N.26.d.4.0.20.) The relief was complete by 4 P.M. One Company of 9th N.F. relieving our "B" Company at N16.c. and a detachment from 9th N.F. relieving our detachment at MAIERE CAVES	
	15 16 17 18 19 20th		The Battalion lay in HENIN CAMP doing as much training as was possible in view of the day and night working parties which the Battalion supplied every other day. The training included P.T., L.G. firing on ranges, Steady drill, and Rifle Grenade instruction including "Barrage". Units of the Reserve Brigade were ordered to cross to "stand to" in the morning from 15/12/17 but the Battalion held itself in readiness to move at ½ an hour's notice.	20th Draft 49 O.Rs. Joined
	21		Lieut. Colonel Spencer Acklom D.S.O, M.C. (Assumed) Command of the Brigade during the absence of Brigadier General THOMSON D.S.O on leave. Major Allen M.C. Assumed Command of the Battalion during the absence of Lieut Colonel Spencer Acklom D.S.O, M.C. The Battalion relieved the 11th Suffolks in the left Battalion Area in its Right Sector, 34th Divisional front. The Battalion took over the line with three Companies forward ("C" Left; "D" Centre; "B" Right) and One Company ("A") in Support.	Casualties 1 O.R. Wounded.

A.5834 Wt. W4973/M687 750,000 8/16 D. D. & L. Ltd. Forms/C.2118/13.

WAR DIARY
or
INTELLIGENCE SUMMARY.

(Erase heading not required.)

Army Form C. 2118.

Sheet 80

Place	Date	Hour	Summary of Events and Information	Remarks and references to Appendices
	Dec 22		Battalion holds a three company front holding posts manned with small garrisons and Lewis Guns.	
	23		Active patrolling was maintained - by which means we had complete mastery of NO MAN'S LAND. The Enemy was quiet and showed no signs of aggression.	2 O.Rs Wounded
	24		Dawn patrols were sent out to the enemy wire daily to ensure that no offensive measures were in preparation on attack pending.	
	25		The Battalion was relieved by the 20th N.F. and became the Battalion in Support with H.Q at the NEST, One Company in EGRETTRENCH - the NEST and FOSTER AVENUE, One Company in EGRET LOOP, one company at the ROOKERY and one Company in CONCRETE RESERVE.	1 O.R. Wounded
	26		The Battalion - during this tour Constructive Consecutions what were	
	27		placed in the wire in front of the RESERVE LINE by the Reserve	
	28		Battalion under this supervision of our Officers. Several working parties were also found.	
	29		The Battalion relieved the 20th N.F. in the left Battalion Area of the CENTRE Sector 34th Division of Area. The line was taken over as before with three companies forward (A, B and C) and one company in Support - (D Cy)	
	30		Listening patrols were sent out at night and the usual dawn patrols at 6 a.m.	3 O.Rs Wounded
	30		Southern & Consecutions Constructed by day were put out at night in addition to the	Draft 27 O.Rs. Joined

3rd BATTALION TYNESIDE SCOTTISH,
(22nd (S) Bn. NORTHD. FUS.)

WAR DIARY or INTELLIGENCE SUMMARY

Army Form C. 2118.

VOLUME 25.
Sheet 81. 22NF

Place	Date	Hour	Summary of Events and Information	Remarks and references to Appendices
CUCKOO RESERVE O.25.c.10.35.	1-1-18		The Battalion held a line Company front - as follows Rt. Fwd. Coy. "B" Coy.; Centre Fwd Coy "A" Coy.; Left Fwd. Coy. "C" Coy.; "D" Coy. was in Support in MALLARD RESERVE. The weather continued to keep very cold and the hardness of the ground together with the snow made patrolling difficult. Advanced sentry posts were established, and a dawn patrol furnished by each Company went out as far as the enemy wire.	2/Lt E.L.O. BADDELEY transferred to 2nd Middlesex 1-1-18
	2-1-18		The Battn. was relieved by the 20th N.F. and moved to SHAFT AVENUE where it became the Battn. in reserve.	
SHAFT AVENUE	3-1-18		Companies reconnoitred their battle positions in accordance with DEFENCE SCHEME. Working parties were found at night for work in the forward area. An officers reconnoitring patrol under 2/Lieut. ANDERSON reconnoitred the SAP at the head of BLOCK LANE in O.32.a.	
	4-1-18		A further working party of 100 men was found by the Bn. by night.	
	5-1-18		The same number of men went on working parties by night. The patrol of 2/Lieut. ANDERSON was repeated.	
CUCKOO RESERVE	6-1-18		The Bn. relieved the 20th N.F. in the LEFT CENTRE SECTOR. 34th Divisional Area. One fighting patrol and two reconnoitring patrols were sent out in addition to the dawn patrols. The fighting patrol under 2/Lieut ANDERSON	

WAR DIARY or INTELLIGENCE SUMMARY

Army Form C. 2118.

Sheet 82.

Place	Date	Hour	Summary of Events and Information	Remarks and references to Appendices
	6-1-18		engaged the enemy but was unable to secure any identification.	2/Lt E. HARLAND joined 7.1.18
		7.15	The situation remained very quiet. The usual reconnoitring patrols were	
		8.15	found nightly and the usual dawn patrols - by each forward company	1 O.R. Wounded 9.1.18
		9	scoured front and main set'ts causing travel to Battn. and making some	
			movement practically impossible.	Joined 10.1.18
		10	The Battalion was relieved by the 20th N.F. and took over the position	2/Lt N. DAVIDSON – E. KENRADE
			vacated by the 20th N.F. in Brigade Support as follows:– "A" Company EGRET LOOP;	
			"B" Company CONCRETE RESERVE, "C" Company one platoon – NEST, one platoon EGRET	Joined 12.1.15
		11	TRENCH and one platoon CUCKOO COURT; "D" Company CUCKOO RESERVE.	2/Lt M.D. HODGE
		12	During this tour in SUPPORT the Battn. found night and day working	
		13	parties for work in the forward area. Owing to the sudden change in the	Joined 13.1.18
		14	weather and the exhausted condition of the men there was an unusual number	2/Lt J. ROBINSON – L.W. LOADMAN – A.E. NEILL – R. PEARSON – J.M. MARSHALL
			of sick.	
		14	The Battalion relieved the 20th N.F. in LEFT of the CENTRE SUBSECTOR	
			as follows: RIGHT FWD. Company. "D" Company; CENTRE FWD. Coy. – "A" Company;	
		15	LEFT FWD. Coy. "B" Company; SUPPORT – "C" Company	Joined 16.1.18
		16	The usual night patrolling and work – wiring were carried out.	2/Lt G. APPLEGARTH – R. BEGALLON
		17	The Battalion was relieved by the 20th Bn. N.F. and became the	
			Battn. in Brigade Reserve in SHAFT AVENUE	2/Lt P. DEIGHTON
		18	During this tour the Battalion provided day and night	to Sept. ?? Sec. R 1/B
			working parties.	

A 5834. Wt. W4973/M687 750,000 8/16 D. D. & L. Ltd. Forms/C.2118/13.

WAR DIARY
or
INTELLIGENCE SUMMARY.
(Erase heading not required.)

Army Form C. 2118.

Sheet 83.

Place	Date	Hour	Summary of Events and Information	Remarks and references to Appendices
	Jan.19		Every man in the Batt. had a bath - his under clothes changed & his uniform cleaned. Sick parades continued to be abnormally big on account of the exhausted condition of the men. Although all precaution were taken several cases of trench feet occurred.	Draft 27 OR joined 19.1.18. 2/Lt. G. KEENAM to England sick 19.1.18.
	20		The Battalion relieved the 20th NF and became the Battalion in the Left Subsector as follows; RIGHT Coy. -- "B" Coy., CENTRE Coy.-- "D" Coy., LEFT Coy. "C" Coy., SUPPORT Coy. "A" Coy. The usual reconnoitring patrols were sent out nightly. The work	Quiet. 1/OR to OR hospital.
	21			
	22		has principally cleaning trenches and wiring. Dawn Patrols reconnoitred the enemy wire every morning.	1 OR wounded w.1.s.18
	23		The Battalion was relieved by the 20th NF, and became the Battalion in Brigade Support as follows:- CUCKOO RESERVE ---- "C" Coy. CONCRETE RESERVE ---- "B" Coy. EGRET LOOP ---- "D" Coy. EGRET TRENCH NEST CUCKOO PASSAGE } ----- "A" Coy.	
	24		The Battalion found working parties for the forward Battalion.	
	25		The Division began to be relieved by the 3rd Division and moved to Corps Reserve in the GOMIECOURT area. The Battalion were relieved by the 1st Battalion N.F. and moved to	1 OR Wounded 25.1.18.

Army Form C. 2118.

Sheet 84

WAR DIARY
or
INTELLIGENCE SUMMARY.
(Erase heading not required.)

Place	Date	Hour	Summary of Events and Information	Remarks and references to Appendices
NORTHUMBERLAND LINES near MERCATEL.	Jan 26		The first day was devoted to cleaning and reorganisation.	
	27		Programme of training was commenced including:- Physical Training - musketry - Arm drill - slow and quick marching.	
	28		WIRING - BOMBING - LEWIS GUNS and GAS instruction in the CROISILLES sector were necessitated in accordance with	
	29		The line in the CROISILLES sector were necessitated in accordance with	
	30		Corps defense Scheme.	
	31		Enemy raids were carried out nightly, but no damage was done to NORTHUMBERLAND LINES.	

CrAllen Major
Commanding 3rd BATTALION TYNESIDE SCOTTISH
(22nd (S) Bn. NORTHD. FUS:)

22 NF
VOLUME 26
Sheet 85 9/11 26

WAR DIARY
INTELLIGENCE SUMMARY
(Erase heading not required.)

Army Form C. 2118.

Place	Date	Hour	Summary of Events and Information	Remarks and references to Appendices
NORTHUMBERLAND LINES MERCATEL	FEB 1st		Programme of training was continued throughout the morning and interplatoon sports were played in the afternoons. Special work was done in the revetting of parapets environ	
	2nd			
	3rd		the huts, as a precaution against enemy bombing. Daylos officers & men joined the Battalion as the result of the Reorganization of the Battalion was employed in night working parties on	
	4th			
	5th		the nights of Feb 3rd 5th and 7th in digging the HENINEL	
	6th		Sunken. This made it difficult to carry out the programme	
	7th		of training in the morning. There was however Battalion	
	8th		drill after the execution of parapets served the link was continued under Company arrangements.	
	9th		The 102nd Brigade commenced to move by inward route via G.H.Q. reserve. The Battalion marched to BLAIRVILLE and	
BLAIRVILLE	10th		encamped there for the night	
GOUY en ARTOIS			The Battalion marched to GOUY en ARTOIS and encamped there for the night	
MNIZIERES	11th		The Battalion proceeded to its destination in G.H.Q. Reserve	

Army Form C. 2118.

WAR DIARY
or
INTELLIGENCE SUMMARY.
(Erase heading not required.)

Sheet 86

Place	Date	Hour	Summary of Events and Information	Remarks and references to Appendices
MAIZIERES	Feb 11th		and occupied billets in the village of MAIZIERES. Brigade H.Q. was situated in the next village of AMBRINES	
	12th		The day was devoted to cleaning.	
	13		The hours of training were devoted to P.T. Bomb Drill, L.G. instruction, musketry. Practice with Egg Grenades and Rection Drill	
	14		"C" Company was allotted the range and fired gun fire practice	
	15		"A" and "B" Coy. (less Lewis Gunners and men to Refreshment Group Practice) were allotted the Range for Application Practice at 100 yds. and 200 yds. Lewis gun teams were under R.E. instruction. Lewis Gunners paraded under the Adjutant	
	16		The Battalion were again allotted the Range which were used by two companies. The other two companies continued training. The Divisional Commander paraded the Brigade model to the Teams which had successfully pulled all other teams compete in the Divisional competition	
	18		Battalion Drill and kit inspection were carried out.	

Army Form C. 2118.

WAR DIARY
or
INTELLIGENCE SUMMARY.

(Erase heading not required.)

Sheet 87

Place	Date	Hour	Summary of Events and Information	Remarks and references to Appendices
MAZIERES	Sept 18		The Battalion was visited by the Tyneside Scottish Committee	
	19th		The morning was devoted to Battalion Drill aio "trang". The afternoon was spent in platoon inter platoon football matches and bayonet.	
	20 21 22 & 25		The mornings were devoted to battalion drill, firing on the range, bombing and tactical manoeuvres, and lectures. The sports programme was continued in the afternoons	
	26		The 102nd Bgde was inspected by the Corps Commander	
	27		The Battalion moved by march route to BERLES - AU - BOIS	
BERLES ERVILLERS	29		The Battalion move by march route to BELFAST CAMP ERVILLERS The Battalion Tug of War Team pulled and won the Corps final on 29/9/15.	

Spencer Wilson Lt Col
Comma'dg 3rd BATTALION TYNESIDE SCOTTISH
(22nd (S) Bn. NORTHD. FUS:)

34th Division.

102nd Infantry Brigade.

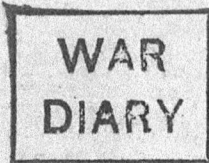

WAR DIARY

22nd BATTALION

NORTHUMBERLAND FUSILIERS

MARCH 1918

Army Form C. 2118.

WAR DIARY
or
INTELLIGENCE SUMMARY.
(Erase heading not required.)

Sheet 2.

Place	Date	Hour	Summary of Events and Information	Remarks and references to Appendices
BELFAST CAMP	March 11th		Second and Third Battle Stations and Complete Kit inspection was held and as much training as possible was carried on in the morning.	Lt Lewis W.E. to England for duty 15/2
	12th to 18th		The Battalion moved forward to its assembly position in the Corps line and Headquarters were in the road 200 yards S. of St. LEGER. Men were billeted. The Battalion was employed in Rifle grenade instruction. Lewis Gun classes and working parties were carried out by day. The Battalion found working parties by night in the forward area. Continual daily reconnaissances of alternative positions in case of enemy attack were carried out by all Officers.	
	19th		The Battalion went with the rest of the Brigade, again taking over the right Sub-sector of the Right Brigade in the Divisional front. The disposition of companies was as follows:- Right forward Company "C" Coy., Support Company "D" Coy., Left forward Company "A" Coy., Reserve Company "B" Company.	Left 6:30 pm 7/3/18 Arrived 2/5 13/3/18
	20th		Enemy attacked. His barrage opened at about 5am. and was very intense - particularly on the Support trenches, Lewis and BUNHILL ROW. It consisted of H.E. and GAS. The initial casualties on account of	
	21st			

Army Form C. 2118.

WAR DIARY
or
INTELLIGENCE SUMMARY.
(Erase heading not required.)

Sheet 5

Place	Date	Hour	Summary of Events and Information	Remarks and references to Appendices
U25.b.55.25	March 21		*(continued)* they were keen	Casualties Lt.Col. Ashton Killed
		11am	The Right forward company formed a defensive flank on the Battalion on our right had been forced back. Two platoons of the Reserve Company were sent to extend the flank westward	Missing Capt. Brown J.Q. 2/Lt. Davidson H. " Beatie G.H. " Carter S.E. " Grant J.H. " Prescott B. " Kinsey J. " Robinson H. " Odell F.J. 2/Lt. Faulkes H. " Bagg A. Jp.
		11.30	Two rifle sections of the Reserve company were sent forward to assist the forward company.	
		1pm	162nd L.T.M.B. section reported that the enemy were in ECOUST. One Company 25th N.F. was ordered to extend the defensive flank westward along the ECOUST SWITCH to Left Bn. H.Q. at U25.a.60.60 Battalion H.Q. moved	Wounded Capt. Bixby R.H. 2/Lt Anderson C.S. " Moore W.J. " Leach A.C. " Sexton R.S. Capt. Bryan E.J.S.
U25.a.60.60		1.30	- The enemy gained a footing in the front line & the Right forward Company as far North as G.O.G. and endeavoured to work Northwards but were held up.	Other Ranks Missing 446 Killed 30 Wounded 69 545
		3pm	The enemy was reported to be on the HOGS BACK. Two Companies 25th N.F. were immediately ordered by Brigade to counter attack.	
		4pm	The enemy were seen advancing on the HOGS BACK towards CROISILLES	
		5pm	The enemy was seen getting in on the W. side of the Railway bank at between U25.00.90 and U24.d.55.60.	

Army Form C. 2118.

WAR DIARY
or
INTELLIGENCE SUMMARY.
(Erase heading not required.)

Instructions regarding War Diaries and Intelligence Summaries are contained in F. S. Regs., Part II. and the Staff Manual respectively. Title pages will be prepared in manuscript.

Place	Date	Hour	Summary of Events and Information	Remarks and references to Appendices
	March 21	5 p.m.	The Left Company practically intact and the remainder of the three other companies made a fighting retirement Northwards on to a line from FACTORY AVENUE to CROISILLES SWITCH-NORTH. When the enemy were on three sides, three Lewis Guns and	
		2200	its H.Q. personel of 22 N.F, 23 N.F. and 25 N.F. made a lendeavor redoubt of Batt's H.Q. whilst all documents were burnt — and then a fighting retirement was effected Northwards. The remains of the Batt. together with parties of 23 N.F. and 25 N.F., T.Coy R.E's, and 102 Pioneer Company held the CROISILLES SWITCH NORTH. The enemy attempted to enter the trench N.of St. Leger. In the afternoon the enemy entered St. Leger and flank fighting ensued. The Battalion was relieved at night and returned to	
MOYENVILLE			billets at MOYENVILLE	
ABLAINZEVELLE	23rd		The Battalion moved by march route to ABLAINZEVELLE where it occupied huts for the night.	
BAILLEULMONT	24th		The Battalion moved by march route to BAILLEULMONT where it was billeted for one night.	

WAR DIARY
or
INTELLIGENCE SUMMARY.
(Erase heading not required.)

Army Form C. 2118.

Sheet 5

Place	Date	Hour	Summary of Events and Information	Remarks and references to Appendices
BEAUFORT	25th		The Battalion marched by march route to BEAUFORT where it was billeted for one night.	
VILLERS L'HOPITAL	26th		The Battalion marched by march route to VILLERS L'HOPITAL and billeted there for one night. The Battalion provides piquets to guard the Southern approaches of this village.	
	27th		On the night of the 27th the Battalion entrained at FREVENT and proceeded to STEENBECQUE.	
TANNAY	28th		The Battalion detrained at STEENBECQUE and proceeded by march route to TANNAY where it billeted for one night.	
AARREWAGE	29th		The Battalion proceeded by march route to AARREWAGE where it was billeted for one night. A strength of 140 O.R. arrived.	
ESTAIRES	30th		The Battalion proceeded by march route to ESTAIRES and were billeted for one night.	
ERQUINGHEM	31st		The Battalion proceeded by march route to ERKINGHEM where the Brigade became the reserve Brigade to the division in the line. A strength of 106 O.R. arrived.	

W Brown Capt.
Commdg. 2/2nd Dr. Mortd. F.W.R.

34th Division.
102nd Infantry Brigade.

22nd BATTALION

THE NORTHUMBERLAND FUSILIERS

APRIL 1 9 1 8

34th Division.
102nd Infantry Brigade.

WAR DIARY

22nd BATTALION

THE NORTHUMBERLAND FUSILIERS

APRIL 1 9 1 8

22nd N Fus
Sheet 6. Vol 2.
Vol 28

WAR DIARY / INTELLIGENCE SUMMARY

Place	Date	Hour	Summary of Events and Information	Remarks and references to Appendices
ERQUINGHEM	April 1st		Battalion forms part of Corps Reserve. Responsibility - Support of Right Division. Intention of Right flank of Right Division in event of enemy's attack developing on the front of Portuguese Corps in conjunction with XI Corps, support the Portuguese in preventing the enemy from covering the front - LYS & LAWE. Reconnaissance of Line R.4.a. 9.9.2.9 surrounding country allotted to 22.N.F. and carried out by Coy. Comdrs.	Capt. R. Bobby D.S.O. Rejoined 1-4-18. Draft 30 O.R. joined 1-4-18.
	2nd to 5th		Reorganisation of Battn carried on which special reference to training of Lewis Gunners. Men were tested. Reconnaissance by Company Commanders. Special attention paid to discipline of new draft. They were well disciplined and a good class of young lads - their musketry excellent.	2/Lt. C.L. Eludd H.R. joined 10-4-18. Draft 159 O.R. joined 2nd
HOUPLINES	5		Battn. relieved 11th Suffolks on the LEFT (HOUPLINES) subsector of Divisional Front.	
	5th 6th 8th		Our patrols were very active particularly during dawn periods in view of known intentions of enemy to prepare for attack. New Outpost line laid down & resisted were reconnoitred & wired. These were slightly withdrawn and an old front line was patrolled by fighting patrols day & night.	
	9th		Enemy attacked Division on our Right after heavy gas bombardment of Armentières during the night - the gas smell strongly in our sector. A Coy was ordered to support the Right Battn. which had sustained heavy casualties owing to gas.	

WAR DIARY
or
INTELLIGENCE SUMMARY.
(Erase heading not required.)

Army Form C. 2118.

Sheet 7 Vol. 3.

Place	Date	Hour	Summary of Events and Information	Remarks and references to Appendices
HOUPLINES	9th	4/am	Enemy made progress on Right Flank. Right 9/10th Battn. Leics was heavily bombarded with Gas (Mustard) and H.E., and gas masks had to be worn about 3 hours.	Casualties: Major Birtle Scott killed 13th Capt. Bobby Syd killed 13th Capt. Hardy C.E. killed 13th 2/Lt. Dunn M. killed 9th Capt. Weir F.L. wounded 13th 2/Lt. Mara F. wounded 13th 2/Lt. Hodgson B. wounded 13th 2/Lt. Hartnell E. wounded 13th 2/Lt. Cockburn Col wounded 13th 2/Lt. Hartley L. wounded 16th Capt. Wintrop (R.A.) wounded 9th 2/Lt. Valentine F.C. Messing 13th 2/Lt. Nisbett G.R. Messing 13th 2/Lt. McLaren W. Missing 13th 2/Lt. Grundy S.H. wounded 20th
		10a	Enemy attacked on our LEFT Flank which was covered by the river LYS and flooded area.	
		12 noon	Enemy had made considerable progress on both flanks. To attack developed on our front which, being lightly picket with H.E. Orders were issued for a withdrawal to take place at 3 p.m.	
		3 p.m.	Battn. withdrew under 7 Coys. D.C.B. B. Coy. formed the rearguard for the Battn. Enemy fire increased during the withdrawal which was however successfully carried out with few casualties. The line of withdrawal was along the main NOUVELLES HOUPLINES — ARMENTIERES Road. The mist prevented low flying enemy planes overhead from observing our withdrawal.	
		5:30 p.m.	Battn. reached outpost position about 500 yds. N. of POINT DE NIEPPE. B. Coy. came under M.G. fire from the South whilst crossing the River LYS. D. Coy. found it impossible to take up positions indicated owing to heavy M.G. fire and they withdrew their left flank and B. Coy. (in reserve) was brought up on their left to form a switch from the NEIPPE system to the River LYS facing NORTH.	
	11th		Night passed quietly. Large numbers of stragglers known through all posts. At dawn enemy commenced this attack pushing up white lights as the signal to start.	

Army Form C. 2118.

WAR DIARY
or
INTELLIGENCE SUMMARY.

Sheet 8. Vol. 2.

(Erase heading not required.)

Place	Date	Hour	Summary of Events and Information	Remarks and references to Appendices
NEIPPE	11		Enemy appeared to be attacking from the South & gained PONT de NIEPPE & opened heavy fire with M.G.s in our rear - cutting off our way of withdrawal. C Coy. was detailed as rearguard to cover our withdrawal to NEIPPE system at about 6.30 a.m. The withdrawal of A.B. & D. Coys. was effected without heavy casualties but C. Coy. found it impossible to withdraw after holding the enemy. Practically the whole Coy. became casualties to enemy M.G. fire.	Casualties o.r. killed 12 wounded 111 Missing 322 Reinforcement 9/5/20 =
		9 am	Enemy low flying plane appeared dropping signal lights which were enabled from the ground. It flew over our lines and was immediately brought down & crashed by rifle & L.G. fire. Later another plane flew low & was fired at, and he made for his lines appearing to be in difficulty. During the day enemy artillery fire increased until in the evening it was very intense & his artillery followed his infantry at remarkable speed.	
		7.30 p.m.	Enemy put down barrage of 5.9's, whizz, and attempted to advance in small groups but was unable to make any progress owing to our rifle M.G. fire which was kept up until about 9 p.m. to cover our withdrawal which took place at 8.15 p.m. Enemy M.G. patrols were encountered during the withdrawal, endeavouring to cut off our retreat. These were successfully engaged & several wounded prisoners taken.	
			The Battn. assembled on [?] the BAILLEUL - NEUVE EGLISE Road returning (first for 3 days) & had a few hours rest.	

Army W. W1289/M1297 75,000. 1/17. D. D. & L., Ltd. Forms/C2118/14.

Army Form C. 2118.

WAR DIARY
or
INTELLIGENCE SUMMARY.

Sheet 9   Vol. 2.

(Erase heading not required.)

Instructions regarding War Diaries and Intelligence Summaries are contained in F.S. Regs., Part II. and the Staff Manual respectively. Title pages will be prepared in manuscript.

Place	Date	Hour	Summary of Events and Information	Remarks and references to Appendices
STEENWERCK	12th		Just before dawn the Battn moved to support the troops holding the Right Defensive Flank N. of STEENWERCK. Day was quiet.	
		5.30 p.m.	Enemy attacked and succeeded in penetrating but being and A. & B. Coys. were ordered to fill the gap in the vicinity of NEUVE EGLISE. The situation was restored and maintained throughout the night despite many attempts by enemy to establish himself in houses etc. in the vicinity.	
	13th		Our positions throughout the day were heavily bombarded and the enemy was persistent in his crawling forward tactics.	
		3.30 p.m.	Enemy attacked in force, was successfully held but made progress on our left, leaving our flank exposed. Battn Headquarters very heavily shelled. All H.Q. Officers became casualties excepting the Signalling Officer. We were able to cover the gap & establish a strong point and maintain our positions until dark, when a withdrawal was ordered. The Battn withdrew and dug in in support near the Asylum, BAILLEUL establishing outposts at PEWTER FARM.	
BAILLEUL	14th to 17th		Our outposts maintained their positions under heavy fire until relieved on evening of 16th. Battn shelled in bivy and moved into trenches 500 yds. EAST CROIX de POPERINGHE in reserve to line established 1500 yds. E. of CROIX de POPERINGHE.	27 O.R. Joined 16th
	18		Battn relieved front line & outposts in Right Subsector of Brigade front on night 17/18	

A7093. Wt.W12839/M1297. 750,000. 1/17. D.D & L., Ltd. Forms/C2118/44.

Army Form C. 2118.

WAR DIARY
or
INTELLIGENCE SUMMARY.

(Erase heading not required.)

Sheet 10. Vol. 2.

Place	Date	Hour	Summary of Events and Information	Remarks and references to Appendices
MT NOIR NR ABEELE	20		Bn. was relieved by the 401st French Inf. Regt. and moved by march route to farm near MT NOIR thence to near ABEELE.	Joined 22-7-18 Capt Onyons M.S. Lieut Blackrigg S. " Taylor B.F. 2 Lt Nelson G.G. " Ainsworth H. " Dyson L.W. " Black S.H. " Balson B.W. " Egan J.T. " Watson B.
ST JEAN led BIEZEN	22		Battn. moved by march route to ST JEAN les BIEZEN and was accommodated in huts.	
	23		Battn. spent the day in rest.	
	24		Spent in rest	
	25		Battalion "Stood-to"	
A.16.D.	26		Battn. moved by march route to A.16.D to construct trench system, and when passing through POPERINGHE were shelled – several casualties occurring. Day spent in digging. On night 26/27 the Battn. took HILL Left Battn. Sector of POPERINGHE LINE. On night 27 7/28 Battn. relieved 9th N.F. in BRANDHOEK line.	
	27 28		Battn. heavily shelled in BRANDHOEK line sustaining several casualties. 2Lt Egan J.T. Wounded.	
	29 "		Fairly quiet	
	30			

Commdg. 22nd Northd. Fus.
Lt. Col.

102nd Brigade.
34th Division

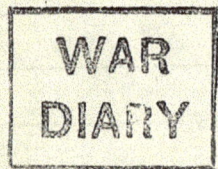

22nd NORTHUMBERLAND FUSILIERS.

MAY 1918

Army Form C. 2118.

22 NF Diary Vol. 3
WO 29

WAR DIARY or INTELLIGENCE SUMMARY.
(Erase heading not required.)

Instructions regarding War Diaries and Intelligence Summaries are contained in F. S. Regs., Part II. and the Staff Manual respectively. Title pages will be prepared in manuscript.

Place	Date May	Hour	Summary of Events and Information	Remarks and references to Appendices
BRANDHOEK LINE	1		Battalion was in Reserve and held BRANDHOER LINE	
	5		Battn. was relieved by 10th Lincolns	
	6		Battn. relieved the 15th Royal Scots in POPERINGHE LINE	
	7th/12th		Battn. was relieved by the 15th Royal Scots in POP. LINE and moved by march route to Camp near ST. JAN TER BEZIN. Training carried on — special attention being paid to Bn. Staff Instructors	Capt J W Ashburner Rejd. 12-5-18 Capt. Old Marshall Killed Jnl. 12-5-18
ZEGERS CAPPEL	12		Battn. moved by march route to ZEGERS CAPPEL, ROSROUCK area.	
	13		Battn. entrained and moved to COULOMBY moving from there by march route to LOTTINGHEM.	To Base 15-5-18 Lt Oldham 8/10 Lt Hardwick Col Buddy 9/7 Lt Cain P.O. " Batcar 90 " Dunscomb P.R.
LOTTINGHEM	14/6		Time spent by Battn. in training and cleaning up.	
	16			
	17		Battn. was relieved in establishment to form a Training Cadre in order to train American Troops. Surplus personnel proceeded by train to Base for reporting	
BECOURT	18		Battn. Training Cadre moved to BECOURT to make arrangements for billeting and training 1st American Battn.	2nd Lt Cain 90 " Dinsmore P.R. 2 63 other Ranks
	25		Bn. Embarkation proceeded to 101st Bde.	Major M Willgey rejoined 25 5/18
	to		One Company of Training Cadre was affiliated to 1 Battn.) American Infantry	
	31		H.Qrs who affiliated to Regtl. H.Qrs 109th Inf. Regt. 55th Brigade.	
			A. Coy " " " " " and formed a Regtl. School	
			B. Coy " " " " " to 1st Bn.) 109th Inf. Regt.	
			C. Coy " " " " " " 2nd "	
			D. Coy " " " " " " 3rd "	

W Symmers Major for Lt Col.
Commdg 22nd North'd Fusiliers

102nd Brigade.
34th Division.

Battalion transferred to 16th Division 17.6.18.

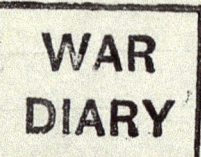

22nd NORTHUMBERLAND FUSILIERS.

JUNE 1918

Army Form W.3091.

Cover for Documents.

R

Natures of Enclosures.

~~Miscellaneous~~

~~Intelligence Summary~~

102nd Bde
Operation Orders &c.

Notes, or Letters written.

S E C R E T.

34th DIVISION ADMINISTRATIVE INSTRUCTIONS No. 15.

Reference 34th Division G.S. Instruction No: G.S.232/46.

Reference sheet 62.c. $\frac{1}{40,000}$

1. **AMMUNITION.**

   (a) Brigade Dumps will be established as under :-

   <u>103rd Brigade</u> - L.26.d.1.1. - JEANCOURT.
   L.23.b. central.
   <u>101st Brigade, attached Troops and Divnl. Reserve.</u>
   L.11.b.3.3. - The EGG.
   L.5.d.2.8. - HARGICOURT.

   (b) The Dump at the Cross Roads in K.12.d. will be taken over by Divisional Headquarters on the 20th as an Advanced Divnl. Dump, and may be drawn upon in case of emergency.

   (c) The Main Divisional Bomb Store will be at K.30.a.2.7., as at present, and units will normally draw therefrom by 1st Line Transport. During operations bombs, etc., will be issued on demand.

   (d) The contents of the various dumps etc., are as in the attached statement, Appendix I.

   (e) Indian Cavalry Dismounted units may draw either from the Right Brigade Dump at JEANCOURT or from the Main Divisional Bomb Store.

   (f) S.A.A. will be drawn by Brigades direct from the D.A.C. The Divisional Machine Gun Officer will indent direct on the D.A.C. for S.A.A. for the Machine Gun Squadrons and Machine Gun Sections working under Divisional control.

2. **SUPPLIES.**

   (a) Troops taking part in the attack, will carry, "on the man", rations for the day of the attack, and the "Iron Rations".
   Rations for subsequent days will be sent up by the usual method.
   Pack saddles may be demanded from D.A.D.O.S. up to 60 per Brigade if required.

   (b) Reserve rations will be maintained at the Brigade Dumps as shown in the Appendix "I".

   (c) A half ration of Rum for issue to troops taking part in the attack, may be drawn from S.S.O. under Brigade arrangements, and issued to the troops on the night of the attack.
   A half ration of Rum may also be drawn under Brigade arrangements for issue on the night subsequent to the attack to troops who have taken part in the attack.
   This applies to both Phases "A", "B", and "C".

SECRET.

APPENDIX - "B"

PROGRAMME FOR THE DISCHARGE OF GAS.

From 0 to 0.4. Four cylinders "White Star" per bay.

" 0.4. to 0.20 One "Red Star" per emplacement every 10 minutes.

1.20. All remaining cylinders to be turned on. This will entail 12 "White Star" and 8 "Red Star" per emplacement.

The discharge of gas to be accompanied by heavy shrapnel barrage on front trenches and bombardment of communications.

To cover the noise of the initial discharge the G.O.C. 101st. and 102nd. Inf. Bdes. will arrange for the fire of Machine guns all along the line just prior to and during the initial stages of the gas discharge.

On the termination of the discharge of gas the following rocket signals will be fired from USNA and TARA redoubts commencing at 1.28.

Three pairs of RED rockets from each post at 30 seconds interval between pairs.

The G.O.C. 102nd. Inf. Bde will arrange for the firing of these rockets. They will only be fired provided the discharge of gas has taken place.

SECRET.

APPENDIX - C.

1. If the wind permits discharges of smoke will take place during the last 10 minutes of all the concentrated bombardments which are to be carried out on V.W.X and Y days.
The barrage will start simultaneously at the following times:

    V. day.   5-10 pm. to 5-20 pm.
    W. "   10-10 am. to 10-20 am.
    X. "   5-40 am. to 5-50 am.
                6-50 pm. to 7 pm.
                7-10 am to 7-20 am.
    Y day.   5-10 pm.to 5-20 pm.

2. Smoke candles and P bombs will be used and will be distributed as follows
    101st. Inf. Bde.   624 P. Bombs   (52 boxes).
                            1560 Candles.

    102nd. Inf. Bde.   972 P. Bombs. (81 boxes).
                            2440 Candles.

3. Smoke will be made from 86 points on the front, points being equidistant from one another and approximately 30 yards apart.

4. The number of points from which smoke is to be discharged will be

    V and W days   38 in 101st. Inf. Bde. Subsector.
                        65 in 102nd. Inf. Bde. Sunsector.

    X and Y days.   22 in 101st. Inf. Bde Subsector
                        44 in 102nd. Inf. Bde. subsector.

At each point there will be 1 N.C.O. and 1 man - infantry - (The O.C. 4.Coy R.E. will give such assistance as he is able for supervision.)
The necessary parties will be detailed by the Brigade so as to distribute smoke along the whole Divisional front.

5. Each group will be supplied for each smoke attack with
    4 P bombs.
    10 Candles.

The time table for discharge of smoke will be.

Minutes.	P Bombs.	Candles.
0	2	1
1	1	1
2	-	1
3	1	1
4	1	1
5	-	1
6	-	2
7	-	2
8	-	2
9	-	-
10	-	-

Bombs and candles will be thrown as far forward as possible.

Smoke candles burn for about 2 minutes; P bombs throw out a dense cloud of smoke for about 1 minute and continue to give out a lesser degree of smoke for about 10 minutes.

6. Candles and P Bombs will be issued to the G.O.C. 101st. and 102nd. Inf. Bdes in bulk. They are to be stored in dry dugouts and the candles are only to be removed from these dugouts for use tied up in waterproof sheets.

7. The O.C. G. Coy. R.E. will report to G.O.C. 101st. and 102nd Inf. Bdes; with a view to instructing prior to U day not less than 2 Officers of each Brigade and the necessary N.C.Os and men as to the method of lighting and throwing P.bombs and candles.

8. The Correct time will be obtained daily by Brigade Commanders from the Signal Companies and the former will make necessary arrangements for communicating this to the front line. Personnel detailed to throw P Bombs and Candles must supplement lack of watches by judging the intervals at which to discharge the candles and smoke bombs.

9. During each smoke barrage every effort will be made to impose upon the enemy that an infantry assault is about to be launched. Dummies will be exposed over the parapet. Careful arrangements will be made as regards the employment of these so as to ensure their having the desired effect. If misused or stupidly used they will only indicate to the enemy that no real attack is intended. Material for construction of dummies is being supplied.

APPENDIX C 1

SPECIAL SMOKE BARRAGE ON Z DAY.

On Z day if the wind is favourable a smoke barrage will be formed as follows:-
(a). Along the Northern face of LA BOISSELLE salient. This barrage to be formed by four 4" Stokes Mortars, 120 bombs allowed.

Emplacements for these mortars have been constructed at X.13.c.8.5. The O.C. No. 5 Battn. Special Brigade R.E. will be in charge of these mortars and will find the necessary personnel.
The Officer in command has been directed to report to the G.O.C. 102nd. Inf. Bde.
(i) The barrage will only be put up provided the wind is blowing from S.W. to N.W.
(ii). Firing will commence at -0.4. and will cease at +0.8.
(iii). No bombs to be dropped North of an East and West line from X.13.c.10.5. to X.13.d.9.7.
(b) Along the Western face, (crater area) and Southern face of LA BOISSELLE salient.
This barrage will be formed by 300 P Bombs.

The O.C. G Coy. R.E. will provide one officer and 12 men to supervise the discharge of these bombs which will be thrown by the garrison allotted for the crater area.

The Officer in command has been directed to report to G.O.C. 102nd. Inf. Bde.

(i) The barrage will only be put up provided the wind is blowing from S.S.W to N.
(ii). The barrage will commence at -0.3. and will cease at +0.6.
(iii). Bombs will be thrown from 12 points on roughly a 300 yards front approximately along the line of TUMMEL STREET.
The Officer of G Company R.E. supervising the operation will decide on exact positions as late as possible so as to take advantage of any slight variations in direction of the wind.
(iv). The following will be the programme for the discharge from each of the selected 12 points.

-0.3 mnts	4 P.Bombs.	Zero.	3 P.Bombs.
-0.2 "	4 "	1 mte.	3 "
-0.1 "	3 "	2 "	3 "
		3 "	
		4	
		5	
		6	

APPENDIX C.
INSTRUCTIONS FOR THE DISCHARGE OF SMOKE.

1. Smoke will be discharged for half an hour commencing at 7-20 am. on Y. day

2. Smoke Candles and P bombs will be used and will be distributed as under:-

    101st. Inf. Bde.   273. P.Bombs. (23 boxes) 1380 candles.

    102nd. Inf. Bde.   528 P.Bombs (45 boxes). 2640 candles.

3. Smoke will be made from 67 points on the front, points being equidistant from one another and approximately 25 yards apart. The number of of points from which smoke is to be discharged will be:-

23 in the 101st. Inf. Bde. Section, 44 in the 102nd. Bde Section.

At each point there will be 1 N.C.O. or sapper of the Special R.E.Coy. & Infantry.

The necessary parties will be detailed by Brigades so as to distribute the smoke along the whole Divisional front.

4. Each group will be supported with :-

    12 P.Bombs. (1 Box) 60 candles. (These will be carried to the trenches in bundles of 36 tied up in a waterproof sheet).

5. Time Table.

    1 P.Bomb will be thrown from each point per minute from 0 to 12.

    2 Candles will be thrown from each point per minute from 0 to 30. Bombs and candles will be thrown as far forward as possible.

6. Each smoke candle burns for about 2 minutes.
Each P.Bomb burns about 1 minute.

7. During the Smoke barrage every effort will be made to impose upon the enemy that an Infantry assault is about to be launched.

  (i). The Artillery will put a barrage on the enemy's front trenches.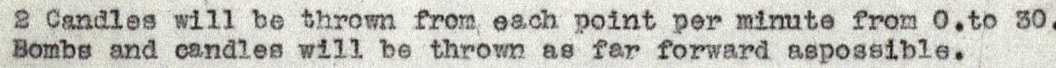

  (ii). Dummies will be exposed over the parapet. Careful arrangements will be made as regards the employment of these dummies so as to ensure their having the desired effect. If misused or stupidly used they will only indicate to the enemy that no real attack is intended.
Material for the construction of the Dummies is being supplied.

www.ingramcontent.com/pod-product-compliance
Lightning Source LLC
Chambersburg PA
CBHW081541160426
43191CB00011B/1806